THE
SILVER
THREAD

*A journey through
Balkan craftsmanship*

ELIZABETH GOWING

To Pamela and Brian
Hoping it brings back
happy Yugoslav
memories

Elizabeth Gowing

For the next generation:
for Adena, Annie, Arabella and Ellie to whom I have been an elusive godmother. You are gorgeous girls and young women whose lives I've been privileged to share.

And for my beloved new nephew, Alexander.

May you all shine!

First published in 2017 by Elbow Publishing

A catalogue record for this book is available from the British Library

ISBN 978-0-9574090-4-0

Cover design by Su Jones and Paddy McEntaggart

Inline photographs © Elizabeth Gowing except where others are acknowledged alongside the photograph

Design and typesetting: Sally Ellis

Printed and bound in Great Britain by
TJ International Ltd, Padstow, Cornwall

THE SILVER THREAD

A journey through Balkan craftsmanship

ELIZABETH GOWING

Thanks are due to all those who are mentioned in the book, for sharing with me the way that silver shapes their lives. I'd also like to thank Michael Koenig and the others who got me to Stan Trg. I am deeply grateful to those who commented on drafts of the text, including the lovely Robert Wilton and the members of my online writers group – Helen Moat, Paola Fornari Hanna, Stephen Fabes, Suzy Pope and especially Moira Ashley who read through the entire book – and the members of the writers group I read sections to in Tirana: Cosmo Kay, Joshua Miekley, Kelly Odor, Kelsey Heeringa, Linda Melbourne, Lori Amy, Matthew Brunwasser, Matty Thimm, Nick Stansfield, Paul Alkazraji, Raena Bailey-Kay, and Stella Rose.

I am very grateful to Hannah Brandley for proofreading the text. To Su Jones and Paddy McEntaggart for such beautiful cover design, and to Sally Ellis for the typesetting I give profound thanks: it is a pleasure to work with people who can weave something almost as stunning as filigree from the medium of ink and paper and pixels.

CONTENTS

Chapter 1. A package arrives in Islington

I lay alone in our bed. Rob had said he would try to call this morning and I knew it would be early because of the time difference, but so far the telephone had been silent. I tried to imagine where he was right now, trying to remember what he had told me about his travels in South East Europe. For years now he'd been studying and working on the literature and politics of the region but I was still struggling to navigate it. I looked along the bookshelves which lined our bedroom and tried sounding out the strange-looking author names. I wished I could get my tongue round the consonants of his world, but the *q*s that were *ch*s and the *j*s that were *y*s defeated me.

I took out his itinerary. He was gone for two weeks which included training on being an election monitor, several days setting up a polling station along with local counterparts (I imagined tough young men in leather jackets, still muscled from their experiences of a guerilla insurgency, and old men with gaunt cheekbones and old-fashioned hats), and a long day of watching voting take place. It was 2001 and Kosovo was about to hold its first parliamentary elections since the war in 1999.

'Is it safe?' I'd asked Rob before he left, and he'd smiled at my nerves. I'd wanted to ask again when he'd called after they'd arrived, but our phone conversation had been full of the honey tastes of the pastries he'd been served, the cobbled streets of the medieval capital where his polling station was situated, the invitations to coffee from the family of his interpreter. It sounded safe.

I hedged the question the next night too. 'How was your day?' 'Fine,' he said, 'until I got a blade held to my throat.'

I felt like there was something in my own throat – the icy press of steel in a warm soft place.

Rob laughed, 'The guy was giving me a shave at the time – an old man with a proper razor. He was working his way around my neck with it and we were making a kind of conversation in the limited German which we shared. He told me he'd been a partisan in the Second World War, fighting with Tito against the Germans. He got a bit lost in reminiscence just as his blade hovered over my jugular.'

My breath came out in a kind of gurgle as if I myself had just had a major artery severed.

'Look after yourself, please,' and Rob promised he would.

But yesterday had been the day I'd been most nervous about – polling day itself. I had imagined ballot-stuffing, intimidation of minority Serb voters, restless queues of men who'd fought a war for their right to vote. The last time I'd seen images of Kosovo it had been during the conflict of 1999, with pictures of refugees on the news and miles of shuffling columns made up of families turned from their homes at gunpoint. The women's faces were tired and fearful, the men's angry and resentful; the babies were sad when they whimpered and even more sad when they were silent.

That had been two years ago – the babies who had been clutched in the arms of mothers in the refugee columns were now walking on their own. The families had returned to Kosovo; the fifty per cent of homes that had been burned during the war were being rebuilt and NATO troops had moved in to make sure everyone felt safe. The mothers who had been wrapped in blankets on that long walk away in 1999 were now back to baking baklava for visiting election monitors to drool over.

'Cold,' he said when the phone finally rang and I had the chance to ask how he was. 'All safe and everything calm. But bloody cold. We're nearly done here, and tomorrow we'll have some time in the city at last, and I've seen something I'm going to buy you.'

He was back in London a few days later. When he walked through the door I rushed to hold him, to check the reality of flesh against the remembered features. His skin was cool and although I knew it was a result of his walk from Highbury station I blamed the Balkans – this war-torn region blowing a chill into our flat. He smiled and stretched out his hand and I felt warmth returning.

In the palm of his hand was a scribble of silver; two intricate chains that coiled and glinted.

'Your present from Prizren,' he said. The place name was unfamiliar and, still looking at the way the necklace and anklet caught the light, I heard it as *prism*. 'The town where we had our polling station was famous for this kind of silver filigree.'

I took the chains and played them between my fingers, like running my hands under a tap. I tried to understand how they had been fashioned, following their spirals and interconnections. It was all I had to understand where Rob had spent these weeks – a slither of silver my only connection to that world.

'They're beautiful; I'd love to know how they were made,' I said.

'Ah, for that we'd have to go back to Kosovo together one day,' Rob said with a kiss as he went to unpack.

Chapter 2. Facing our fears; travels through the history of silver at Trepça

Rob and I were packing. Not just sun lotion and counting-out-pairs-of-socks packing because this wasn't going to be a holiday or a trip you could count out in changes of underwear; this was dusty, turn-your-house-upside-down, arrange-a-garage-sale packing. Five years had passed since Rob's trip to Kosovo. I had worn the anklet under five seasons of summer skirts, had fiddled with the necklace at five Decembers of Christmas parties and smart dinners. As my fingers played, and while I carried on the conversations of my London life, my thoughts would turn to that land which Rob had visited; a country flashing silver with cut-throat razors, vicious winters and emerging democracy.

Fingering the links, I had started to understand some of the techniques which had created the twists and loops of my Kosovan souvenir; the tiny oval cells of silver wire that had been made to be fitted with miniature rams' horn double spirals that reminded me of old-fashioned twin spools of camera film. But what were the tools and machines, what the eyes and steady fingers that could fashion such fine work?

It had been a surprise to us both that I was now to have the chance to find out. A simmering wanderlust had been growing gently in those five years; a sense that other people's souvenirs were not enough and that both Rob and I wanted more than Islington could give us right now. We were in our early thirties and we'd decided we didn't want children;

friends had started asking us what our plans were and I would rub the necklace between my fingers like a charm and explain that we'd applied for voluntary work overseas and Rob had started asking around through contacts he had on Whitehall to see whether anyone knew of an adventure waiting to happen.

At short notice, following the indictment of Kosovo's prime minister for war crimes, a new Kosovan prime minister had been chosen and he'd asked for a British adviser. Rob was chosen for the job and so this morning, ten days after him being offered the position, we found ourselves sticking post-it notes on books: blue if they were to go to Kosovo with us; yellow if they were to stay in storage in the UK. All those ones whose authors' names were unpronounceable were tagged blue. And I had started to learn the Albanian – though not yet the Serbian – alphabet so I could even pronounce some of them correctly now. Later that day the packers would arrive to take our possessions away and in ten days' time we would follow them to the land where silver flashes.

When we arrived we were hosted at a series of kind lunches, barbecues, dinners – as if menus were the best handbook for our new life. In between discussions on the wine (local red drinkable; local white less so) and the beer (local lager excellent except for the experimental pineapple-flavoured version, to be avoided), I tried to turn conversation to my necklace and its history.

People told me that Kosovo's Trepça mines produced lead, zinc, cadmium, gold … and silver. No-one could be sure but everyone agreed that it was likely that it was from the Trepça complex that the silver had been blasted out, refined, extruded, twisted and fashioned into my favourite necklace.

Following up these suggestions with research I discovered that the biggest Trepça mine is just outside Kosovo's ethnically divided city of Mitrovica, in the typographically implausible Stan Trg. Perhaps surprisingly, the typo in Stan Trg is not in the unlikely-looking second word (meaning 'market' or 'square' in Serbian), a growl resulting from the Serbian ('srpski') efficient omission of vowels so that words looked like a txt message on a mobile phone owned by someone parsimonious. The mistake lies in the first word and came about during the paperwork setting up the mine's modern history when it was opened by a British company. At some point in the exchange of memos on the subject, a fly spotted, or a fleck of dandruff fell from an anonymous clerk, or ash from someone's cigarette floated precisely into the space between the final letters of the word '*Stari*' which denoted the 'Old' Market area. It fused the two letters and thus was christened the new and spuriously named enterprise of Sta*n* Trg.

The more I read, the more I wanted to visit this, the rawest of starting points for my necklace. It took a while before I found ways for such a thing to be organised but eventually through a friend I got the contact details for someone who suggested that a trip down the mine might be a possibility. We fixed the date on a Friday for the next Monday and I spent the weekend fretting. I didn't want to call myself claustrophobic, but of all the phobias this, along with what I recognise is an irrational fear and revulsion against rats, was my greatest. I'd had discreet panic attacks sitting in the back seat of three-door cars, and when I'd visited the tombs beneath the Giza pyramids years before I had ended up battling through an oncoming crowd of tourists in a small shaft, muttering incoherently that I needed to get out, need to get out, sorry, need to get out urgently, emergency …

I had been down one other mine – perhaps fifteen years before when I'd visited a disused tin mine in Cornwall which had been converted into a museum. It had been sanitised and interpreted, with postcards available afterwards, but even there I had asked in a breathless rush if we could please abort our trip and go back up to the surface ….

Over the weekend I relived these various experiences that lay on a spectrum from frightening to embarrassing. How would I fare down this mine? I reassured myself that this time I was on a purposeful hunt, to learn the origins of my silver necklace; that would keep my mind busy and stop me musing on the half a kilometre of rock pressing down on me from above. I thought about my friend who has a phobia of flying and how perverse it seemed to me to focus on the number of metres of air beneath you as you sailed through the clouds. With our positions reversed and an excess of rock above rather than air below I resolved not to be perverse about torturing myself.

Arrived at the mine on Monday morning, I was taken in to the director's office. It had all the signs I'd learned to associate with status in Kosovo – a padded door, a desk holding a small cup of Turkish coffee which had presumably been served by the smiling secretary who had led me in, an ashtray filled with butts, and a sponsored calendar (this one from the anti-corruption agency). I introduced myself to Director Qazim Jashari and explained my interest in Kosovan silver, my desire to write a book about its apotheosis in filigree but wanting to track it down here to its very beginnings, hidden in the rock. Qazim's voice was gravelly, as if it was rasping through backfill. He gave me a brief overview of the mine, gesturing to a map on the wall which showed the eleven levels where mining took place. My stomach lurched.

He reminded me of all the things that silver was used for – not just necklaces but nuclear reactors, solar energy and semiconductors, touchscreens and water purification. He also explained the basic process of how silver was extracted – that the ore contained lead, zinc and silver, with the silver combined with the lead. Once the ore was excavated, the lead/silver mix and the zinc were separated off and the remaining slag – which could be as much as ninety per cent of what had been extracted – was returned to the mine as filler for worked-out areas. Of a ton of extracted minerals there might be only one hundred grams of silver. My necklace seemed even more of a miracle than I'd realised, and I imagined the truckload of rubble it might originally have sat in.

The mine worked non-stop, with three shifts a day, and no days off. As well as the men who worked there, there were vital pumps which also laboured without pause. And in a country, and a town, with desperate levels of unemployment (officially six out of ten people of working age in Kosovo are economically inactive), this mine with its 730 jobs was offering local families something as precious as metal. Silver didn't seem like a luxury when I thought about what it was offering the men who brought it out of the ground. And Qazim told me the working conditions here were good, with food provided to every miner at the beginning of his shift, and free transport from five local pick-up points.

Then I was taken to meet the geologists who'd accompany me round the mine. Refik and Xhemajl were initially reserved so I asked them some questions about things I hadn't understood about the mining process – how exactly the bars of silver that could then become fine jewellery could be filleted from out of the earth. They showed me photographs of minerals and incanted names – 'arsenopyrite', 'rhodocrosite', 'sphalerite'. I stumbled over them and they shrugged, 'Of course, you're not a geologist.'

I wondered whether I should tell them I was a claustrophobe, and ask in advance for their help if I needed it when we were underground, but I couldn't bear to lose any further respect from them. Anyway, I wasn't going to be a claustrophobe today. I just wasn't.

I was passed on from the geologists' office to Sherif who would kit me out with appropriate clothes for going down. This felt like a positive step – I was in a short skirt and leggings, with bare feet in blue sandals with delicate silver embroidery, and what had had me feeling pretty and appropriately smart when I arrived at the mine offices was now making me feel uselessly feminine and impractical. 'Do any women work down the mine?' I'd asked Director Qazim and he'd said no, 'it's no work for a woman.'

So it was with some pride that I explained that I had with me in my bag more sensible footwear – a pair of trainers together with socks and trousers. Sherif smirked,

'Trainers will be no good. You'll need boots.' I didn't want to mention that trainers had been fine when we went down the tourist experience mine in Cornwall...

My trousers were also apparently not appropriate, and I was handed a heavy duty pair of standard issue which co-ordinated with the jacket Sherif also gave me, bearing the symbol of the mine with crossed mallet and pick. I had been reading Thoreau the week before this visit and I thought ruefully of his warning: 'Beware of all enterprises that require new clothes.' But it seemed too late to back out now.

I was shown into the changing area which had a couple of shower cubicles hung with incongruous curtains printed with playful dolphins. Leaping around the work clothes hung to either side of them they looked like they were reveling in the fluidity of the elements of air and water. It was almost a taunt to men who were preparing to battle with the toughest parts of the element of earth. Or maybe it was a motivation for them, being reminded of the other world that awaited them at the end of their shift.

All the clothes were too big for me, but with some rolling up this was less problematic than with the rubber boots I was given which were also several sizes too large. I took off the impractical blue sandals and as I tried to negotiate my way into the big boots I wobbled on one leg, trying to keep as much of my foot as possible off the cold tiled floor until Sherif told me to use some of the pattens which lay around. These were crude slabs of wood with rubber loops that looked like they might have been cut from old car tyres. My sandals on the floor beside them looked over-engineered.

Once the boots were on I practised a kind of rolling walk to accommodate the fact that my feet sloshed within the boots but were also weighed down by the surprisingly heavy soles. On an expedition when gravity was already going to take me further than I'd like, I didn't feel the need for such drag.

Sherif led me out to meet up with Refik and Xhemajl standing with other miners at the door where we waited for the lift (which the men referred to as the 'basket') to take us down. I usually avoid taking lifts and instead take the stairs especially when going down. That probably wasn't an option as we set off down a distance equivalent to descending a 130-storey building. Nevertheless, I was thinking about the implications of what Qazim had told me about this lift, received as a donation from America in 1954. Phrases like 'metal fatigue' nibbled at my confidence.

'Here's your helmet,' Refik handed me a white plastic hard hat. 'You should put it on now.' It was tight and my head started to hurt immediately. I wished I'd had something for breakfast and wondered whether any claustrophobe had ever embarked on such a misadvised expedition.

The 'basket' (I thought of the monks winched up to the monastery at Meteora) was taking its time to arrive and I looked around. Above the door we would go through to access the lift was the Trepça symbol I had printed on my jacket, and around it the words '*me fat*'. Looking at the lean, wiry guys queuing with me, it read as an unlikely caption in English. In Albanian it means 'good luck' which conveyed rather more desperation and belief in chance than I liked from the engineers I was relying on here. I looked away and out across the valley where the mine sits. For the site of such famously polluting extractive industries, this valley was notably lush and wooded.

On the opposite side of the valley I noticed a blocky building which showed clear signs of bullet damage.

'What's that building?' I asked an older man next to me.

'It was where the workers lived before,' he said. 'The Serbs (he used the offensive term for them, 'shkijet') did that during the war. They took this place over. When we came back to it we found what they'd done here – ropes in the basement where they'd tied people up, and we found signs they'd been raping girls here too.'

I never found any other references to these rapes, but I felt these unnamed girls, and all the other victims of war, hovering over my view of the site. This was rapidly becoming a nightmare. And it was only going to get worse if I went down; I turned to Refik, 'I think…' I began, and was then cut off by a clunking and screeching.

'The basket's here,' said Xhemajl, putting one hand on my shoulder to politely let me go in first. The other miners waited courteously behind us.

'What were you saying?' asked Refik standing back to let me pass.

'Er … nothing,' I said with a gulp as I took a wide unsteady step across the threshold which gaped with 805 metres of black space, to reach the swaying metal box punched with crude uneven holes for air. I stood with my back to the rear wall and the other miners pressed in front of me. This didn't seem to be the time to mention my claustrophobia either.

I concentrated on breathing. I told myself that as long as you keep breathing steadily then there is nothing claustrophobia can do to you. With rattles and clangs, the door was shut and our tin can of men started its controlled fall downwards. I soon discovered that here breathing was not reassuring. There was an oily metallic tang to the air, and I remembered where this air was coming from – that it was a belch tinged with cadmium and lead as well as silver. I tried thinking about my quest instead – about tracking the silver down to its very beginnings. It would be worth all this.

Somewhere off to the side there was the deep resonance and whoosh of another lift in action. 'That's the ore,' Refik told me – 'it goes up as we go down'. I thought of us counterweighting those tons of stones, and in each of them a few links of future necklaces – or LED chips or X-ray images.

With a jolt we stopped, and Refik and Xhemajl pushed me out into the darkness. My first impression was surprisingly of space and of air, with a distinct draught rushing past me. I had made it! In the basket, down a mine, and ready now to go back up again.

'Thank you for bringing me here,' I said in a conclusory way to Refik and Xhemajl. 'It's so interesting to have experienced it.'

'We're going to walk this way,' they said, ignoring or misunderstanding my hint. And they set off.

There was nothing for it; I followed them even though each step took me away from the basket and my only way up to the world. I knew I needed to keep up with them as it would be terrifyingly easy to get lost here. I saw no signage anywhere in my time underground. The landscape was shifting so fast that perhaps it wouldn't have been useful – what was a rock wall today would be a new chamber tomorrow. When Refik and Xhemajl tried explaining to me the topography of the place as it had been at various points in the past I got dizzy. It was the same – or perhaps exactly the opposite – experience I had with architects as they carved possible walls out of thin air, to hear these men talking about carving spaces out of solid rock. Refik told me that you could always use a compass if you were lost, and he got out his smartphone with a compass app to show me.

I had no smartphone, and no compass, so I stuck with him.

I had imagined the mine as a shaft and then a series of caves. I had not been prepared for the spacious underground community in which I found myself. The director had told me that there are a total of two hundred kilometres of passageways within the mine and I realised it would have been better to imagine an underground town. The surface underfoot was uneven, but otherwise we could have been striding along a boulevard. At one point a full-size lorry came out of the darkness at us. We flattened ourselves against the rough walls and it passed on, carrying what Xhemajl said would be ten tons of minerals. Pathways opened up off to either side, and sometimes we passed rooms blasted out of the rock: an office with a desk and a telephone sat on it, wire strung up through the ceiling – and presumably up and up, for hundreds of metres. We passed offices and repair rooms, a rugged hollowed-out resting area, where men sat with sandwiches, which had its parallel in many cosy cafes above ground.

But this was a town in black-out. We carried our light with us in little pools spilled by the heavy-duty torches attached with thick rubber tubes to industrial batteries which we'd all been issued with. The lights sparkled and glinted on minerals studding the walls and ceilings which surrounded us. Sometimes looking up was like staring into the Milky Way. I was disappointed that the lights didn't come mounted on our helmets but Refik explained that only those who needed their hands free to work were given the headtorches – we wore ours strung round our necks like stethoscopes. Where there was light, there was life, and as we peered into the galleries and anterooms and alleys and sidestreets it was only if we saw the bob and lurch of answering torchlight that we knew we had company.

When you came up closer to the people strolling these streets the lighting became more problematic; the beam was too bright to be able to stare it out so each person gave a courteous dip as cars do with headlights. It meant that conversations were carried out in chiaroscuro. Perhaps it was this, or perhaps it was poverty and hard-living, but the faces of every miner we met seemed chiseled and gaunt;

cheekbones sharp as quartz, and ragged smiles gleaming like calcite formations in dark faces.

The conversations were brief – greetings by name and short questions as to whether work was going OK. Invariably they began or ended with the same slogan I'd seen painted above the entrance to the mine, '*me fat*,' and an answering, 'Yes, *me fat*'. I asked Refik about it and he explained that when you were in the mine there was no morning, no afternoon or evening – for shift-workers far from sunlight the usual greetings weren't appropriate. 'And it is just luck – whether you are in the place where there's a cave-in, whether there's bad gas … so it's luck that we wish one another.' My claustrophobia seemed a rather bourgeois concern alongside this ready living with the real possibility of death.

But the phobia was still present, like a gentle squeeze around me that I knew could tighten – if I let it. And we'd been walking for perhaps twenty minutes now. Walking away from the lift shaft ….

'Are we going to have to walk all the way back again?' I asked in a small voice.

'Well, we're going to go down the big ramp to the next level,' Xhemajl explained. 'And then we'll walk back again along the way we've walked, but one floor down.'

'And how much longer will it be before we get to that ramp?' I asked.

'Not long now,' Refik reassured me. 'Are you tired? Would you like to stop and rest?'

No, no. Let's not stop, please. But if I'd known this was the plan I'd never have agreed to come down here. With renewed stumbling speed, I carried on along the dark passageway, away from the lift.

The walking surface varied. At its best it was more or less even and more or less dry. Mostly it was pitted and rutted from the traffic of machines. Usually we could walk along rails put in place in order to get the excavated ore out, and walking along the rails ensured we kept to the centre of the path and avoided the nasty bits of old metal which curled and gnarled out of the wall, many at head height. In places there was water which came almost to the top of my boots and in other places a claggy silt. I was very glad I hadn't worn my trainers, though the boots had grown even heavier from the weight of clay that had stuck to them.

Water was bafflingly present all around me. I had imagined that this would be an exploration in the opposite element – in the solids of the world. But I remembered the pumps which Qazim had mentioned evacuating 3500 litres per minute. There was the sound of hissing and rushing all around. Some of it came from a pipe which ran along much of the rock wall we were following – the hydraulic system operating the drills the miners used. Once as we turned a corner we got a glimpse of the water gushing towards the reservoir from where it would be pumped out. At other times Refik pointed out the path that ancient waters had carved, in soft rounded formations clearly distinguishable against the jagged gashes of manmade incisions. Xhemajl said that when you saw such potholes you knew that there would be precious ore nearby. Under the play of our torches the roof above us was sometimes revealed to have Gaudiesque ventricles formed by steam jets, millennia before. Through them gleamed fleshy swellings slick with damp. If we really were in the bowels of the earth, manoeuvring like a surreal endoscope, these were the tumours we were navigating.

Other growths appeared, and these really were vegetable and soft – sprouts of mushrooms which glowed white when our torches caught them. I wondered whether anything else lived here, other than fungus and miners.

'Just rats,' said Xhemajl. 'But we're glad to have them because when we see them rushing out of somewhere we know that there's danger there.'

Just rats. My terror was complete.

At last we got to the spiral ramp which took us down a gentle incline for an additional depth of sixty metres, the equivalent of perhaps eighteen storeys, to the next level of the mine. Once we'd done that we were walking back towards the lift shaft and I started to relax. I even stopped occasionally to ask questions about the processes that were going on around us. When we saw lights approaching in the distance my heart didn't lurch with the fear that these were going to be people we'd have to talk to, taking up more time than I had left before my demons won the battle raging somewhere around my solar plexus. One old man stopped to say hello and we all muttered '*me fat*' in the approved way. Refik and Xhemajl explained that I was their guest and introduced the old guy.

'What do you think of it here?' he asked me.

'A bit scary,' I said in a gasp of honesty. Refik and Xhemajl looked at me and laughed blithely as if they didn't believe me.

'Oh yes,' the old man agreed. 'I've been working here for 42 years.' It was as long as I'd been alive. 'I remember coming on my first day when I was still in high school, and when I got home my father, who was a miner, asked me how the visit had been. I told him, "I'm never going down there again" but the next day here I was, and I've been working here ever since. You get embedded here,' he explained. I thought of him like a piece of marmatite fixed in the rock. The Albanian word he'd used for his 'embedding' comes from the word for 'meat' as if he and the mine had actually become one flesh; a grimy, gritty symbiotic sinew.

We passed guys drilling deep into the rock and Refik explained that they were making the holes where explosive would be inserted – one every ninety centimetres – and detonated at the end of the shift once all the other men had left the mine and before the next shift came in to start carrying away the pieces of ore that resulted. Later we passed a metal door set back into the rock wall.

'That,' said Xhemajl, gesturing with his cigarette, 'is the explosives store.'

I told myself that we must soon be back at the lift shaft. Any return journey usually seems shorter than the outward leg because you can pace yourself. But even though we were traversing the same distance – only one floor down – the dark tunnels still seemed almost endless. I no longer thought I was going to faint, but it did occur to me that others must have done so at some point. Not rookie visitors perhaps, but workers suffering a heart attack or breaking a leg, or otherwise taken ill. How on earth would they be got out? I asked Refik and he answered elliptically, 'it's better not to have an accident. Safety is our number one priority.' I resolved that I would definitely not faint.

And then ahead we saw the lift shaft. A small group of miners was waiting at the door. We greeted them – '*me fat*' – and they pressed the buttons in a specific configuration to communicate with the operator at the top. The director had told me that knowledge of the signals to operate this lift was something required from every miner before they were allowed to enter the mine; this could save your life.

Back in the basket, my heart lifting in something between palpitation and exhilaration, the miners asked about me. How long had I been in the country? What did I think of the mine? When I'd given my answers one of the older guys, gap-toothed, fished in a pocket. He brought out a fist-sized lump of mineral and turned it over to catch the lights from our torches. At the bottom was the gleam of pyrites, fools' gold (in Albanian, more politely, 'false gold' – attributing the misunderstanding to the mineral not the miner), but the top of the chunk was what I thought I recognised from my lesson in the geologists' office as sphalerite, the mineral in which zinc is most often found. The men seemed impressed that I'd remembered, and Refik preened a little at the effective teaching he'd given, and the miner with the uneven smile extended the lump to me. 'It's for you,' he said, presenting it to me like an award. I remembered that Kosovo's first President, Ibrahim Rugova, was famous for presenting visiting dignitaries with samples of Trepça minerals. But I bet none of them had ever received their gift as they sped through the Kosovan earth; I rubbed a thumb over the blunt crystals in my hand, wondering whether I could spot a grain of silver somewhere, and feeling genuinely honoured.

After the visit to the mine I was offered lunch by Halil Qela, the former director of the mine, now director of research and development. He told me something of the other history of the silver I'd seen being blown up, dragged out, melted down, and sifted away. He'd worked at the mine since 1987, though like other Albanians in socially-owned enterprises he was forced out of his job in the 1990s. After the war in 1999 he hoped that he and the other miners would return to work, but it took years – surely more years than it should have – before arrangements were made. Indeed, in 2003 the miners went on what he describes as a twelve-day 'strike' to lobby for the right to return to work. By then three of Trepça's seven mines were under water. Of the others, two were in the north and under separate Serb control. In the control of the Kosovan authorities there remained only Stan Trg and the Novo Brdo mine. Finally, normal work resumed in 2006 though the mines are still owned by the Kosovo Privatisation Agency, and the hunt for investors is ongoing. Among possible suitors was Prince Michael of Kent who came to Kosovo in 2010 with a delegation of potential investors investigating what was, at least until the Kosovan war, the third largest smelting capacity in the world, and where it's reckoned that there are still 4,500 tons of silver waiting to be extracted.

Halil took over as director in 2012, as the miners' choice, as he told me proudly. He talked about the need he immediately identified to co-operate with his counterpart in the northern part of the mine complex, and how on his first day of work he'd called the Serbian director a few miles away and, speaking the Serbian he'd learned fluently at school, said that he was willing to work together. The Serbian director had answered that if he really was, then he should prove it by coming straight over to the Serbs' office. Halil said he'd known he needed to prove his sincerity. Wary of possible political fallout if the meeting became known, but also nervous of his personal safety in the tense environment between Serbs and Albanians in Mitrovica, he told only his assistant about the impromptu meeting, with a warning that if she didn't hear from him within twenty minutes she should go to the police.

Halil said that at this point he'd not been to the north of his city for 23 years, and now there was a barricade that needed to be passed. The Serbian director said he'd send a car to collect him once he crossed the river so that he didn't have to try to pass in a car with Kosovan numberplates.

'I was… I wouldn't say scared. But… scared,' he said. Having beaten my claustrophobia that morning suddenly seemed rather a pathetic achievement.

The tension and the personal leaps of faith necessary for making Kosovo work became obvious as he told me the story of that day. He was greeted by his counterpart at a café, where he was presented with a closed bottle of juice to serve himself from. His mind running on poisoning, Halil said he saw this as a question of trust, and he told the Serb that he didn't need a closed bottle; he'd take a cup of tea, 'to show my confidence that I would be looked after.'

In the end, he stayed for six hours, being taken out to lunch in a restaurant where he recognised dozens of old miners he'd worked with before the war and who came over and greeted him. Halil said that he and the Serbian director agreed they needed to focus on the areas they had in common.

'I told the Serb guy that on the way to this meeting through the streets of Mitrovica I must have seen a hundred people who looked hungry,' he said. 'And I told him that in the south we had people who were hungry too, so what the two of us should focus on was making the mines a workplace for the breadwinners for those families.'

So that is where Kosovan silver comes from. It's born in fear and hard graft, dizzying depths and glinting rocks. It's born from unlikely political alliances and men trusting one another despite the odds. And somehow they emerge – those one hundred grams within a ton – and they're refined and transfigured and they form this smooth bright stream I wear around my neck.

Chapter 3. Larger than Paris; Novo Brdo

Mining had left its traces – and sometimes its scars – on Kosovan culture and countryside for hundreds of years. As I spent more time in Kosovo I learned that the impact of the silver was not just in the lives of Refik and Xhemajl and their colleagues underground.

One of the volumes which had been an indisputable blue-tag in our allocations in London was the deceptively-titled *Kosovo; a short history* by All Souls Fellow, Noel Malcolm. I sifted for the silver thread running through its many pages – reading about silver being mined during the Roman period, through the lavish medieval Serbian kingdom (images of frescoes in UNESCO World Heritage Site Orthodox monasteries) whose wealth was largely dependent on Kosovo's mines in a place called Novo Brdo which Malcolm described as 'one of the richest places in southern Europe'. In its day it was larger than Paris.

A place larger than Paris in its day. As we drove nearer I tried to imagine a medieval Galeries Lafayette and wondered at the cosmopolitan centre we'd be visiting. According to the map we should be close now, and I looked for the sprawl of this ancient town. I could see nothing, though there was definitely high ground ahead. As we approached it became clear that the hill held ruined fortifications, rising impressively out of the surrounding farmland. But where was the town, where the shops and cafes? As we reached the end of the road, with the broken wall of the old castle towering above us, it was conclusively clear that this was Paris no longer.

Novo Brdo's hoard of silver lay mainly in the mines which are still operational there, but others have been unable to believe that there's not more. In 2005, four Polish police officers, stationed in Kosovo with the UN Mission in Kosovo were reported to have been caught searching for archaeological treasure using metal detectors within the walls. They were apparently challenged by Kosovan police and refused to hand over the objects they had uncovered, which included coins.

However, I wasn't here for this kind of silver. After surviving my ordeal at Trepça I wasn't going to go down a mine again, but I was interested in seeing the area where the silver came from. We had come at a weekend and there was no activity in the mine but we were let in to see the buildings and the mine entrance with the familiar '*Me fat*' slogan over its entrance. In the changing rooms the miners' uniforms were hung eerily from the ceiling, suspended with a pulley system which I assumed was to stop petty pilfering. I remembered the bags of food I'd seen at the Stan Trg mine, hung from nails in the wall. Perhaps when you work in the unknowable dangers of depth then there is a particular psychological resonance of the safety in hanging things high up. And I realised with a shudder that of course it keeps them away from the rats.

These mines are famous for theft on a grander scale than pickpocketing or even speculative use of metal detectors. They even got the medieval King of Rascia name-checked by Dante in *The Divine Comedy* for his counterfeiting. The medieval region of Rascia included modern-day Kosovo, and the Serbian King Milutin who ruled it minted his imitation Venetian silver coins here in Novo Brdo. The fakes contained only seven eighths as much silver as the real coins and were banned by Venice.

Driving on from the mine we approached the castle itself. One wall was almost entirely intact, rising up to a height of several storeys and flanked with two towers. There was a cross picked out in red bricks within the stonework of the castle. Clambering up to the walls we found that we could get right up to the castle. Despite the experience with the Polish police officers, there seemed to be no guard, no ticket office, no interpretive signage. It was liberating. I have spent too many days at English Heritage sites squinting at maps and trying to work out which direction is North East so I can understand the information I've been given about the people who lived here. Now I was squinting still, but it was with the upward look of the imagination, trying to visualise the medieval people who'd inhabited this castle; looking out at the view they'd have looked out over, except with houses then where there were now fields and scrubland. I imagined the miners I'd met in Stan Trg and dressed them in fustian instead of acrylic, equipped them with compasses rather than compass apps, and took away their hydraulic drills. Other than that it was the same – the same basic process of men pitting themselves against rock; men taking their chances on rockfall and bad gas because of the possibilities of what could be gained – blasting and burning at the jagged edges in the hope that that spoonful of silver would emerge in each wagonload of rubble.

Looking out over the rolling landscape there were specks of enterprise to be seen emerging from the stones and fields today too. We'd been told about the rural tourism initiative here funded by the Dutch Embassy in Prishtina, and had researched in advance on their charming website which in ambitious English described the opportunities available nearby for the visitor. Each section was followed by a link you could follow to make a reservation. A local guide offered tours not only of the castle but also of a local *teqe* mausoleum, 'a gem in the old town that wil bring you luck, if you walk three times around it. There is a speciality for all those man out there who are not married yet. Turning a tile on the roof of the mausoleum will help you finding a bride! Click here to check availability.'

I never found out whether Rob clicked, but he had suggested we could spend the night together somewhere near the castle, and with more winking exclamation marks the website assured us that this would be possible. So when we'd scrambled down from the ruins we headed for the first house we could see. A rustic board outside proclaimed in English, Albanian and Serbian that this was part of the rural tourism initiative. The house was modern and had a suburban feel to it, with a neat-as-a-pin front garden with its turf distinguished from the rough scrub of the surrounding fields by a wire fence. Perhaps there were still some people living in Novo Brdo who remembered the days when their city was larger than Paris, and this was the ghost-suburb of a ghost town. Opening a small gate in the fence we made our way on teeny-weeny stepping stones across the shaved lawn to the front door. I felt like we should be singing 'hi-ho, hi-ho.'

Inside there was indeed a competent homemaker but she had fewer than seven unruly miners to look after. Our hostess, Fejmja, had married into the eponymous Novoberdaliu family who'd lived on this land for two hundred years, and I was once again reminded that however many layers of laminate flooring the house-proud Fejmja laid down for her home, this was very old land, and that it had been yielding its very old ores for a very long time.

In Fejmja's comfortable spare bed we slept like very old people – long and deeply. In the morning we were offered a hot drink, but I was interested in visiting another rural tourism initiative nearby that a friend had told me about where I had heard we could have our pick of teas. We'd arranged to meet up with our friends Alisa and Burim Berisha and their five year-old daughter, our goddaughter Adena, since they'd said they were also tempted by the idea spending of a summer's day sipping tisanes.

Xhema (whose name is pronounced 'Gemma', perhaps appropriately for someone living in the lands where precious things are dug from the earth) has a smallholding a few kilometres from Fejmja and it was there that we were promised hand-harvested teas.

Although the winding roads confounded Rob's natural GPS, and the absence of any homesteads or passers-by removed the possibility of my usual crowd-sourced alternative for finding our way around, we managed to meet up with the Berishas. Driving on together we finally saw another weather-beaten wooden board from the same Dutch Embassy project and as we pulled up off the mud track, a face that matched the board appeared over the fence. Xhema had a Don Quixote moustache and a sun-dried face. He came out to greet us and I explained that we had come to try his teas.

'We're not serving guests at the moment,' he said mournfully. 'The tree-houses are under restoration.' The non-sequitur sentences sound quixotic too, but soon he elaborated, 'we built these tree-houses for guests to drink their tea in. But the ladders are rotting.' We looked up and saw what he was referring to. The shafts of the ladders had never been straight, having been formed with the natural curves of branches he'd cut. But now there were some unnatural curves in the runners that had been roughly nailed between them. I saw splintering, and thought of little Adena's femur…

However, Adena had stopped listening at 'tree-houses' and was already set off with the five year-old's scorn for gravity or rot. I hastened behind her, ready to offer arms for a catch if persuasion away from the beckoning branches failed.

Somehow she made it up the rickety ladder so I followed, and we managed to lever ourselves onto the boards set out in the branches of the tree. Inside, it smelt warm and sappy. Twin beds were made up and Adena and I caught each other's eye. We would love to spend the night here, soughing between the leaves.

We shuffled carefully out and dangled our legs over the side of the platform, looking down at the rest of the group below us with the foolish pride of people who have made their way up a half-rotten ladder and not yet got down. But it was a dizzying perspective in the same – or exactly the opposite – way that the mine had offered me a new view of the world.

Below us, the grown-ups were taking photographs of Xhema's orchard with the strange fruit budding in its boughs, and Xhema was now asking if we would stay as his guest, reciting names of herbal teas – hawthorn leaf, elderflower, sage, nettle, primrose, strawberry, linden, milkweed, wild apple, saffron, St John's Wort ....

Of course we said yes, and once Adena and I had wobbled down the steps Xhema's wife offered to show me where the teas were prepared, and ushered me in to a room of warm, dry heat and fragrant dust. Piled in the middle was a bloom of elderflower, recently picked. It would soon be laid out on large wooden frames of mesh and put into a roaring rush of warm air. She opened up the metal cupboard where herbs were turned into tea, and with its multiple layers sprouting smells of remembered summers and small dry petals it reminded me of the flower press I had as a child.

Then she escorted me outside and went to see to the boiling, and before long we were all seated in front of little golden bells of tea. It was served in typical Kosovan tea-glasses, as seen across the Balkans – fine tiny tulip-shaped glassware which tinkled in carillon as we all stirred. I joked that we should each sip different amounts and we could tune the glasses properly and play out a melody. The tea had a woody acridity which made me sure it was good for me, and it certainly put me in meditative mood, watching the miniature blonde whirlpool made as I stirred. I thought about the other golden streams threading their way through this zone – the precious metal that Novo Brdo was once famed for.

Xhema told us about his family's history here and the rise and fall of Novo Brdo. 'There's hardly anything left now,' he said, 'except the charcoal. They still produce that even though it's not needed for smelting the silver any more. It's still useful for barbecues,' he smiled ruefully at a town that had once mattered to Dante now slipped to providing only for picnics and the unsuccessful pilfering of expat policemen.

I was interested to see this one further legacy of silver – and the uses for trees when they were not being spliced into play houses – and asked Xhema more about the charcoal. He was an enthusiast, whether he was talking about the purity of milkweed or carbon. I learned how charcoal was used rather than wood in smelting because it burns hotter, cleaner and more evenly. It's produced by leaving wood to burn for days in a low-oxygen environment (covered pits, called *clamps*). The steam rose from our drinks at the table, and I heard with fascination about the intense temperatures that could be produced from this basic industrial technique.

'Go the other side of the hill and you'll find the village of Brus where you can see for yourself,' he said.

So when our tea was finished we drove in search of smoke. I knew very little about the process that would make it but as we wound round the hill and high into woods, we started seeing piles of earth which were covered with branches and emitting wispy puffs and plumes. These were the clamps. I had thought they would be attended by blackened workers, remembering what I'd been told about the stools that charcoal-burners sat on which had only three legs so that you had to keep awake to keep your balance, as a measure to ensure the constant watchfulness necessary from the men guarding the fires day and night. But the smoking here continued unobserved despite being set in highly flammable woodland. Later I learned that the woodland location was not a perverse carelessness of health and safety regulations but a deliberate siting to protect the clamps from the wind. Nevertheless, I felt that a few pairs of eyes – if not legs – would have been no bad thing.

We saw not a soul as we drove on through the blighted forest, and the quest felt increasingly futile as I struggled to understand this one further link in the chain of what silversmithing had brought to Kosovo. I'd seen Paris reduced to rubble, and instead of the glittering fairytale I'd hoped for here, the rough abandoned mounds of dirt gently steaming in the middle of the trees were most reminiscent of the leavings of some vast, vile incontinent creature striding the woodland. Had silver brought Kosovo nothing more than a few fragile necklaces and this?

Larger than Paris; Novo Brdo

Chapter 4. A clearing in the jungle; the silver that the British found in Mitrovica

'Of course it was the silver mines that gave Kosovo its first golf course,' said the British diplomat over lunch when I was talking about my silver hunt. It felt like the sort of conversation Foreign Office types have been having in dusty towns for centuries.

We forked cannelloni stuffed with pungent local cheese and some of the fragrant tomatoes whose delicate flavour reminds you that tomatoes are really fruit, and he went on, 'It was organised by the Scottish manager at the mine owned by the British company, Selection Trust, in the 'thirties. I guess he made sure to have about him all necessary home comforts.'

After the lunch I started the Balkan traveller's bible, Rebecca West's *Black Lamb, Grey Falcon*. It's a beautiful book, albeit one in need of a good editor, which narrates her 1937 visit to the region, including two days in Stan Trg as the guest of the Scottish manager known with the Serbian word for 'Mister' as 'Gospodin Mac'.

I wondered whether any of the guys I'd met at the mine would know what traces were left by this period of silver's history in Kosovo. Halil, the director who had taken me out to lunch, confirmed that yes, the British had started up this mine and built the community around it. 'They had a better nose than others,' he explained, as if silver was something that could be sniffed out like truffles.

Refik, who'd guided me underground when I'd visited, told me that his colleague Abdullah had grown up near what was called the Kolonia Angleze (the 'English colony') further up the valley from the modern-day mine I'd visited. However, he doubted I'd be able to see much there. 'It was damaged during the war, and people have rebuilt houses on the site of the old ones,' he warned. But the idea of an English colony built on Kosovan silver was too intriguing to miss.

I caught a bus out to Mitrovica, set as Rebecca West describes it 'at the threshold of the warm, broken Serbian country that reminds Somerset men of Somerset and Scots of the Lowlands … where the land burns in summertime like the human skin.' From here I took a taxi and met with Refik, Xhemajl and Abdullah at the gates of the Trepça mine. They had something wrapped in sheets of A4 paper which they presented to me.

'I wanted to get some of these for you when we were down the mine,' said Refik, 'but I forgot my hammer.' I opened the pages and found crystalline lumps of grey and white and pinky brown, some bristling with needle crystals. Refik and Xhemajl took a teacherly pride as I recognised the rhodocrosite. I remembered West's comment, '"Everybody likes the Albanians," that is universally said.' I felt lucky in my company as we drove off together a few kilometres further up the valley.

We parked and Abdullah said he'd take us to where the golf course had been. It was a cool July day and we walked past blackberry bushes and elderflower, and we could have been in a British summer. I thought of Gospodin Mac and the little England (the 'Nova Scotia'?) that had been built here ninety years before.

First of all we passed the swimming pool. Abdullah was still swollen with remembered pride about this pool. He was in his early fifties, I guessed, but he had vivid memories of how the swimming pool had been. 'It was the only one in Kosovo,' he said. 'All the tournaments were held here.'

He was talking about a time when Trepça was not just the industrial heart of Kosovo but a significant centre for all Yugoslavia. By the 1980s Trepça employed 20 000 workers, and accounted for seventy per cent of all Yugoslavia's mineral wealth. Abdullah was swimming here when Mitrovica wasn't a divided city. He was talking now about days when the river separating the Serbian north from the Albanian south could not only be easily crossed on unbarricaded bridges; it could be swum. And days when not only his city but his country was warm, fluid and connected, not trapped in a chilly frozen conflict.

'You'd come in here,' he gestured at a young apple tree. 'And here there were ten male changing rooms and ten female changing rooms. The guard sat here …' he kicked at some brambles.

'How can he remember?' mused Refik.

'And how does he know how many girls' changing rooms there were?' I asked.

But Abdullah was still narrating the summer of his boyhood, 'And then you'd take your position …' he gestured at the diving board whose anvil-shaped concrete pedestal still overhung the great blue expanse of the pool.

Except …

The swimming pool was empty now of water's cushioning welcome. Following Abdullah's narrative I thought of diving into it, but the explosion of liquids that would follow would be the liquids of blood and brain. This was now a dangerous place.

We made our way by crumbled steps into the shallow end and walked along the bottom, trampling rubble and drifted litter underfoot on the floor where the golden-limbed boys of a previous generation had dived for coins or for glory.

There was a slow seepage of greenery across the pool now; a gentle tide of weeds and grass that would eventually flood it once again. A sapling was growing out of the wall; a reflection of its roots digging into the concrete seemed etched on the wall in a network of hairline cracks. In perhaps forty years the space would be indistinguishable; the surrounding trees would have matted and overhung it and only the occasional hiker would chance upon some stark lines of the sloping sides or the curved plinth of its diving board like Mayan architecture in a rainforest, and wonder at the rites that once went on here.

Rebecca West had described the community she visited here as 'a clearing in the jungle hewn by pioneers'. Now the pioneers were gone, the jungle had returned.

There was a tennis court higher up the hillside, again cracked and crumbling, with rough edges that would thwart even a deft serve. West mentioned the Stan Trg mining engineers playing tennis, and I imagined them here, freshly bathed after a day in the mine's seamy silvery embrace, darting about in whites, with wooden racquets.

We walked on and Abdullah took us to a rough field. It was scented with marjoram and mint, and scrubby bushes grew across it.

'The golf course,' he announced.

I laughed politely at his joke.

'Really,' he assured me.

I wondered whether this was a fantasy golf course. There's no tradition of golf in Kosovo, though there now is a mini-golf range near the ominously named 'International Village' outside Prishtina. Maybe Kosovars didn't know what a golf course would look like, I thought – perhaps they imagined it like a field for football; any space where a ball could be followed. But as we walked on across the 'links' I noticed shapes in the scrubby grass – areas of sand and small unnatural hummocks. Perhaps it really could have been a golf course. Remembering West's descriptions of Gospodin Mac's dynamism it seemed plausible.

I pondered the figures he and his fellow golfers would have cut, pacing intently across the Kosovan sward with strange shaped bits of hickory, and tonking diminutive balls into place. I imagined the local farmers and miners watching them, bemused, as they congratulated one another at the end of 'a good walk spoiled'. I thought about the cannelloni I'd dined on with that British diplomat and about 'home comforts' and comfort zones, and how there had been no Kosovars in that restaurant where we'd eaten so well, and probably no Kosovars treading this fairway either.

Further down the valley were the Selection Trust era workers housing blocks, unmistakably Scottish in building style, with sturdy walls built with chunks of grey-brown stone reminiscent of Edinburgh. The blocks were now converted into social housing for families from the Mitrovica municipality, and washing was strung between apartments. Faces of old women and children stared dully out at us from windows. I felt like greeting them '*me fat*' as if we were still underground; they probably needed more luck than the miners who had their free meals and transport and jobs and purpose. The small kiosk shops here were mostly empty or half-empty; the place asleep.

We walked down past some houses which were certainly newer than those that Rebecca West would have seen. But I was happy to notice that they were surrounded by beehives, remembering that West mentions the mine manager having been a keen beekeeper.

A few reminders of a more powerful past remained in the abandoned former mining administration block which had an art deco detail in the two long thin windows of double-storey height at its entrance. On its wall was a plaque written in Albanian, with the star of socialism atop it, commemorating the formation of Trepça's first trade union and the strikes organised there. It was dated 1966 and couldn't know then what such strikes would do to Yugoslavia when the Kosovan independence movement which gathered pace during the 'eighties was played out even underground. In 1989 the Kosovo constitution – which in 1974 had won autonomy for Kosovo within Yugoslavia – was rescinded, placing Kosovo back under Serbia's authority. Kosovo Albanian miners tried to use their position to protest against these moves and about 1,350 Trepça miners began an underground hunger strike on 20 February 1989 calling for Kosovo's autonomy and for 'brotherhood and unity'. After ten days, the only strikers left were the fifty who had barricaded themselves inside the Stan Trg mine. In a midnight operation, the Yugoslav Special Anti-terrorist Unit descended through the fire escape shafts and arrested the strikers. The aspirations for Kosovo's autonomy, and wider calls for full independence, had to wait ten years.

During that time headline-grabbing massacres and daily small injustices were committed by the Serbian authorities against the Albanians. So much for what Rebecca West had reported the mine manager having said in 1937, 'The Serb administrators all get to like the Albanians and less and less make a distinction between them and their own people. This country's getting over its past nicely.' I wondered how many times we would have to go through this cycle of men telling such truths to their grandchildren only to have the grandchildren prove them wrong.

As if as a reminder of good times that cannot last, below the former administration building – just down the hillside – was the old wheelhouse with the machinery still visible through its sunken and weather-shattered roof. This was where my countrymen had entered the Kosovan earth down a shaft, similar to how I'd travelled on my visit to the modern mine further down the valley.

Minerals call to people from deep within the earth, and their summons had been heard by people from around the world. I thought of those medieval Saxons who'd shaped the Novo Brdo landscape, and then the British of just a few generations ago who'd restarted the digging, who'd retied the silver threads running through this land to connect the rock with the craftsmen and women who could turn it into something shimmering round my own neck.

However, the building's wreckage, with a roof absent in some parts and badly buckled in others, was a physical representation, above ground, of the travails of the mine and its underground treasures in the time since Rebecca West's social call. Just two years after her jaunt, the Second World War broke out and soon Kosovo fell under Axis control. The Trepça mines were taken over by Goering's private company and they were used for the production of U-boat batteries – this remote inland town powering the crafts which prowled the Atlantic, pluming the oceans with destruction which nearly cost the Allies the war, which kept bananas out of the hands of my father until well after peace was declared; Yugoslav miners half a mile down into the planet's solid rock, digging for the metals to keep their German occupiers safe while deep in the planet's waters.

With one hand touching my lucky charm silver necklace I gazed down into the chasm of the earth at the seams which had tangled through Kosovo's turbulent history after the 1999 war, playing their part in the battles of the 1980s, as well as the battles which had embroiled my own country and my own family in the 1940s, and the bold opportunism and plus fours of the British of the 1930s. Remembering West's description of that era I recalled that she described seeing here 'a goods tram loaded with lumps of ore, the colour of ageing and desperate silver, puffing away.'

Where had it gone, that silver? What was done with it? I wanted to follow this silver thread to the point where it had become a tradition from which my necklace was born.

Chapter 5. Sneezing in Prizren

Imagining a bird's eye view across the country I fancied I saw the silver unspooling from Trepça, in gleaming rivulets running down that valley and across the centuries. If each gram could emit a tiny, tinny GPS signal, I wondered what the map of its journey would be like. Much of it would flow out of Kosovo, beyond the Balkans, of course, but other rivulets would stream within this country and pool into workshops where the grams would then again separate, branch, flower...

'Prizren,' Rob had said when he had given me the necklace. The town of the polling station he'd been monitoring was apparently famous for this craft. So if I wanted to trace this thread from the mines and castles and charcoal which had begotten it, it was now to Prizren I should turn.

The town had been the capital of Ottoman Kosovo, only displaced by Prishtina when the era of the railway gave a new strategic and economic importance to straight lines and the towns that lay on the direct route from Thessaloniki to Belgrade. In fact this may have been the saving of Prizren whose cobbled streets were left unblighted by bland government buildings, its citadel with a view of monastery rather than ministry – of its seventeenth century mosque and fourteenth century UNESCO World Heritage Serbian Orthodox church rather than administrative sprawl.

I'd read about Prizren when I was researching my book about Edwardian traveller Edith Durham. Her description of retail therapy there was enough to inspire anyone

I wandered up and down and in and out the long wooden tunnels of the bazaar streets, dark with hot, rich shadow, glowing with goods .... Had it not been for the difficulties of transport I should have ruined myself

I wanted to wander thus. And in particular I wanted to see those glowing goods of metalwork.

In Prizren I was given the names of two filigree craftsmen still active. I wondered whether either of them was the person who'd made my necklace. Now my Albanian was improving, they sounded to me like a comedy duo – the surnames translated as Mr Bean and Mr Okra.

Mr 'Bean' Pasule was in fact a humourless man. But it wasn't his slapstick I had come to see – it was a magic wand I was looking for. He showed me a dull stick of silver. It was as thick as my thumb, powdery and gross. The phrase 'filthy lucre' came to my mind – the brute power of unlovely silver. 'This,' he said, 'is how the silver is when we get it from the mine.' He set it on the workbench with a thud.

Then he got out a plastic box. Inside was a puff of cotton wool and a light scribble of silver wire. With intricate twists and rolls, the silver had been formed into a marguerite inset with spirals.

'And this,' Mr Pasule lifted the pendant out on his scuffed thumb pad and lifted it to me like a butterfly, 'is what we turn it into.'

I looked at him with new respect. He'd told me he was the seventh generation in his family in this craft and perhaps part of what he'd inherited was a subtle streak of showmanship: the transformation of the metal was unbelievable. And even more unbelievable when I thought about the dirty backstory I now knew – the deep dark mines and the rough miners who worked them, the filthy burners that had smelted the silver. But to produce this silver flower ....

I bought a tiny flower pendant from him and took it home as a fragile souvenir; a reminder of what can grow from the dark and dust of Trepça.

Next I arranged to visit Mr Okra. I told him what I'd seen of the other craftsman's beautiful flower arranging and he was not to be outdone.

'Come to our co-operative and I'll show you what we make when we put all those flowers together,' he boasted.

A daisy chain?

No, I discovered. A mosque. A house. An eagle, a Bible cover ... the scope of the projects was vast.

It was a treasure trove that had seemed increasingly unlikely as I'd wandered Prizren's streets. First I had been wrong-footed by the long geographical memory of Kosovo's citizens. One could presumably draw political and historical lessons from the way that directions are given not using north and south or road names, or even landmarks that can be easily spotted, but instead by navigating a city's history. In Prishtina I was getting used to giving instructions to taxi drivers or pizza delivery men to go to the road between the 'former UN building and the former casino'. I'd even watched in wonder one day during the months that road works were underway in the city and seen how pedestrians strode out and cars obediently stopped for them at the 'former pedestrian crossing', now no longer marked with a zebra because the asphalt had been torn up but where everyone knew the black and white lines should be painted.

So when an English woman asked the inhabitants of Prizren for directions to the filigree co-operative it was natural that no-one flinched at giving careful instructions for how to reach a place that hadn't been in operation for a decade. After a long walk I found myself at some ornamental gates. They were wrought iron but twisted as if giant tweezers had worked on the metal just as Mr Pasule had fashioned the silver wire, making spirals and twirls and delicate insect-like wings from the metal. They were also locked shut.

It was doubly galling to find my access to the factory blocked by two butterflies. I rattled the gates a few times against their padlock, as if reaffirming their solidity. I called out but no-one answered.

I rang Mr Okra.

'No, the filigree co-operative is not in the former filigree factory. We're in the former cigarette factory', he said.

Of course.

So now I asked my way to the cigarette factory and eventually found myself walking up the path to a small industrial unit. Broken greenhouses lay off to my left and some leathery leaves were still hung up to dry. In through a door I found myself in the dark. I used my mobile phone as a torch and climbed a stairway to the first floor where a sign sellotaped to the door announced that I had arrived at *Filigran ShPK*… 'Filigree plc'.

In one walk I had travelled from socialist Yugoslavia to the tough realities of a newly capitalist independent Kosovo. There I met Faik (Mr Okra had a given name, of Turkish heritage where it means 'excellent' or 'leader' and despite the talk of a co-operative, he was a clear first among equals) and he told me about the factory whose building I had stopped at. He gestured at the small room where we now sat, with eight men and women bent over workbenches, with tweezers flashing over tiny silver components.

'All of us who are here worked in that building before the war, in one of Yugoslavia's socially-owned enterprises.'

Fatime, the woman next to him, looked up at the mention of the factory. Her lined face had been pulled into a frown over the spirals she was fashioning from wire. Now she gave a smile which illuminated her face like a flash of silver.

'We were like a family there,' she beamed. She said she'd worked at the factory from 1965 until it closed in 2005.

'But it had started to fail long before that,' said Faik. 'We started to lose trade because of the embargoes against the Milošević regime, and after the war all the socially-owned enterprises were offered for privatisation and the filigree factory was bought up and immediately closed by the new owners.'

'But before the war we had a long time of being unaffected by the embargoes and the problems,' Fatime wanted to tell me. 'We earned according to the hours we worked – not the sales; if you worked more you earned more.'

It was an approach which offered deliciously insulated security for workers, as long as it lasted, and ill-prepared them for selling in an open market. I glanced back at the photograph of an almost life-size filigree eagle the co-operative had made, and wondered what market research would say about its chances for take-off.

'Were you making the same kinds of things there?' I asked.

'We didn't make so much for churches,' Fatime said, gesturing at an elaborate construction sketched in biro on cheap paper tacked to the wall, and its silver shadow taking shape in metal form on the table. 'That was because of the attitude of the regime to religion so more of what we made was jewellery.'

I looked more closely at the biro sketches, trying to guess function from the arabesques and spirals. It was Faik who enlightened me – a Muslim politely showing a woman of Christian heritage around faith's furniture. 'It's a Bible cover,' he explained. 'And this will be a crucifix …' he demonstrated how parts being twisted into shape on the table would come together as a cross.

'This is a censer.'

The customers were Serbian Orthodox churches, placing their orders from these Muslim Albanians in a way that ironically had been more difficult for them to do in the days of Yugoslavia, before Kosovo had declared its independence from Serbia.

I took Fatime and Faik back to those days and addressed my question also to their colleague, Bashkim. His name meant 'unity' in Albanian and was part of Tito's famous recipe for Yugoslavia's success – Brotherhood and Unity. 'What was it like?' I wanted to understand what inter-ethnic relations had been and how simmering tensions had been lived before the Yugoslav dream had exploded into a war. I wanted to know how working with silver had shaped these workers' lives, and to see Kosovo's history reflected in metal.

'It was wonderful,' said Fatime. 'There were over 140 of us in the factory. We had excursions to the seaside paid by the factory. It closed for a month in the summer and when you came back to work you got paid for that month too.'

It wasn't quite the prelude to a war I had expected.

'But what about the relationship with the Serbs at that time?'

'It was good. Because there were more Muslims than Christians, the factory didn't work on Muslim holidays, but to compensate for that we'd do the Christians' work for them on their holidays because they didn't get the day off and we wanted to help.'

I gave up. But Bashkim had sensed that I had been trying to get political in my questions. He obliged me by getting political in his answers.

'This was how it was – they asked me for work and I asked them for wages. I didn't care if things were sold or stolen – that was for the state to worry about. Everyone did their own work; the director managed the workforce, politicians worked with politics, shepherds with sheep. But those days are gone because everyone's in politics now and we're all managers even when we're not trained.'

'Now look at us –' he gestured at the ageing population around the table. I realised that in ten years most of them would have retired. 'Where's the younger generation? And even if the government opens professional schools to train them, where will those people do their internships? Where will they be employed? We had a shop but we had to shut it because there wasn't enough trade; now customers just come to buy here. But there aren't enough of them. Modern people want big stupid things, not the traditional things we make.'

Fatime made some remark to him at that and Bashkim responded with animation. I strained to hear what they were saying, before realising that it wasn't my hearing that was at fault – it was my vocabulary; they were not speaking Albanian.

Fatime saw me frowning in concentration and laughed. In Albanian she said,'We were speaking Turkish.'

Around this battered desk there was a spirit of harmony that was either utterly modern – these Albanian Muslim men and women sitting together creating Christian religious artefacts for Serbian churches – or perhaps very Yugoslav. Or was it something older than that; perhaps I was experiencing what were in fact the last days of the Ottoman Empire. Looking up I noticed a picture of Istanbul's Ayasofya/ Hagia Sophia mosque on the wall. It seemed incongruous on a wall in Kosovo and yet seeing it here gave me a new understanding of the ancient lump of stone and dome. The pride of place given to it made me think of it as an omphalos, the navel of the world – the Ottomans' axis mundi. And I wondered how many other homes and workshops around Europe and Asia and the Middle East had a postcard or calendar like this pinned up. The Ottomans had spread from Yemen to Hungary and across the top of Africa. Baku, Baghdad, and

Budapest had all been Ottoman. Here in Kosovo their rule had lasted over 400 years. Was it surprising that the influence lingered? Faik and his colleagues lived in a world where you could still literally navigate in Turkish – other than Cyprus and Turkey itself, Kosovo is the only country in the world to have Turkish as an official language and I had seen on my way here that in this municipality street signs were written in Albanian, Serbian and Turkish.

Faik tried to explain. 'I'm not Turkish; I'm Albanian. But if they're from the city families show how cultured they are by speaking Turkish.' I tried to think of an equivalent in Britain and wondered what an upwardly mobile jewellery workshop (an 'atelier'?) would have sounded like in Norman England.

Whether as demonstration of the possibilities of transformation, or simply to move us off the complicated subject of linguistic identity, Faik offered to show me how the filigree process begins.

'First you have to see how the silver rod is turned into wire.' He beckoned and I followed him out of the workshop. At the door I turned back. Fatime was staring away from the bench. Perhaps she was looking out at the horizon of a 1970s beach holiday. Bashkim had bent back doggedly to his work.

In a smaller, darker room next door to their workshop Faik showed me a heavy machine, green like something army issued, and compact and heavy enough to be part of a war machine. How could this have anything to do with the fine work of my necklace?

Above the sturdy base were mounted gunmetal grey cylinders with grooves of decreasing width. A thick rod like the one Mr Pasule had shown me was passed through these slick and slowly spinning gauges while the smooth handle at the top was set rotating like a capstan to work the gauges. Dribbles of oil pooled under the machine, like the dark saliva of a great masticating animal.

The rod had come out the other side now and Faik passed it to me proudly. However, I was unimpressed. A thick metal stick. It was no less ugly than it had been when it had first been inserted into the maw of the machine. This seemed to bear no relation to the fine jewellery that had been dangled in front of me.

'It's got longer, and thinner, don't you see?'

I wasn't sure that I did.

Once again he fed the stick into the machine and again the machine excreted something that looked a lot like a thick dull rod.

'Watch!' said Faik, seeming to sense my skepticism.

Again the silver was fed in and out, and back in again and once more pulled out. Now there was no mistaking it – the rod was longer and finer, but you still wouldn't call it wire.

Small pieces of silver had sheared off as it was mangled in the machine and silver slivers lay in glittering snow around the base. I thought of the sparkles hidden in the stone mined in Trepça and of all the effort that had taken the ore from its state latent in rock, through smelting and transportation to now being teased into these lengths with their accompanying smatter of silver by-product. Dust to dust.

After a few more extrusions the metal was as thin as a cable, and starting to ply. On the next insertion, Faik was able to bend the end round as it emerged from the back of the machine and reinsert it in the front so the silver looped him entirely. The next time there was play on the wire and a twanging as it sang out from the machine. Soon he asked for my help in gathering the silver, and I clutched at the air, plucking shimmering threads as if I was myself spinning gossamer from thin air.

From one rod of about five centimetres diameter, a skein of 0.25 millimetres thickness had been produced by the grinding jaws of this machine. The physics of it was staggering, but the maths was even more extraordinary. That original stick had now produced sixty metres of wire as fine as horsehair. Now the miracle of the marguerite blooming from the clod of silver looked more plausible. But still, like a child watching a magician, I wanted to know how exactly it was done.

'Can you show me?'

Returning to the workshop Faik showed me how Bashkim took the wire, and some skeins of other wire of different thicknesses. And like God in his workshop on the third day, he began to sketch out the petals of a daisy a little larger than lifesize. He sketched in metal, using strips of silver – tagliatelle, not spaghetti – forming broad ellipses for each petal which he then pinched. When he had eight petals he used tweezers to set them one against another, meeting at the

centre. And there, where God would have sprinkled pollen, Bashkim took a pinch of something and let it fall.

Now I was prepared to believe anything. This was fairy dust?

'Solder,' said Faik unsentimentally. He reached for an object lying on the table, and used it to brush away the stray grains of the silver dust.

'Is that a …?' I puzzled. It had worked like a brush, but now I came to look at it I saw that there was something knuckled and bony in between the hairs. This was no ordinary brush.

'Yes, it's a rabbit's leg,' Faik confirmed, just as unsentimentally. The idea was vaguely revolting but it did nothing to undermine the image of this place as a wizard's workshop. Looking down the table I saw that the rabbit's leg wasn't just one psycho worker's quirk either – there were a few of the withered, hairy animal limbs lying around.

'It's the best thing for catching up the dust.'

When I turned to answer him I found that his colleague was breathing fire.

A butane canister stood next to the workbench and from it snaked a rubber tube which met with a second rubber tube at a small tap. Beyond the tap was a nozzle. Turning the tap to 'on', Faik's colleague had unceremoniously put the other end of the second tube in his mouth and was using his breath to combine with the butane and regulate a flame he'd lit at the nozzle. The man had become a dragon.

The spurt of flame played over the centre of the daisy and the solder melted just enough to weld together the petals. The craftsman twisted the tap back to its starting position and the flame died. He took the tube from his mouth and held up the flower skeleton with the tweezers. It was no longer eight separate petals, all held together now, but it was a sad withered thing, blackened by the heat.

'The acid will sort that out,' Faik assured me. 'But first we have to fill it.'

From dishes on the workbench Bashkim picked curls of wire. Some had been made into spirals, others into the double spirals in tiny rams-horn shapes. There were zigzags and a different, pinched, zigzag he told me was called 'mouse tooth' and wire with twists in it. For the sample he made me he seemed to have decided that the petals would each be filled with one distended spiral. They were lowered into place and then he turned dragon once more, until the spirals were set in their frames.

'Mouse tooth'

'And now the acid,' he hissed. Faik took me back to the smaller room where there were set on the side two containers. Looking closer I saw that one contained Turkish coffee. The other was hydrochloric acid. I winced at the easy mistake you could make.

But Faik knew what he was doing, and did not drop the little flower into the coffee. It would be the kind of mix-up you'd probably only do once in your life.

And after a few minutes he pulled the flower out again. Its baptism had left it with a white shine, gleaming with all vestiges of the burning gone. Faik rinsed it off and laid it in my palm like a coin that had finally become something useful.

I shivered – this room was cold, without the warming fire of the butane and the little tea-glasses radiating their cosy heat, and the multilingual conversations. My own breath was almost dragonlike here, with steam streaming from my nostrils.

We went back into the workshop and I was offered 'Turkish' coffee made on the small gas stove. I don't drink coffee and I thanked them but said I had taken enough of their time. I was feeling the cold and I should get home, but here today I'd had a magical glimpse of the way that silver was shaped but also of the shaping that it did of lives and histories.

I told the workers how much I'd enjoyed my visit and how wonderful their work was. Halfway through my pretty speech of thanks I broke off to sneeze.

The filigree workers all smiled.

'You know what that means?' they asked.

I pulled my coat about me as I refrained from stating the bleeding obvious of what seemed to be rapidly advancing flu.

'It means you'll come back.'

~ THE SILVER THREAD ~

Chapter 6. Mouse teeth and the new directions silver can take in western Kosovo

I wanted to go back. The magicians' workshop had intrigued me and I felt that I could happily sit there for hours watching the silversmiths at work and trying to understand exactly what they were doing to produce such miracles. Now I saw that the world of filigree was much larger than my necklace. But I also wondered whether I could help them. The sheer size of the creations they'd been working on had made a big impact on me … but not in a good way. I thought of Bashkim saying that they needed more custom, and I thought of the 2500 euro price tag on the model of a traditional Prizren house entirely fashioned from silver. What Kosovar had that kind of money? Perhaps those who drove the 4x4s with tinted windows which went too fast down the motorway. But which of those drivers would spend their money on a model of a traditional house? And of the other people in Kosovo with money, what tourist would want to carry something so heavy home in their suitcase?

For people like me, the simple flower that had first entranced me when Mr Pasule had placed it on my thumb – that was something exquisite, light, transportable, affordable …. I wondered what new products could be created using such small pieces to bring custom to the co-operative.

What if the filigree pieces could be displayed on a greetings card? I thought about the economics of the idea and reckoned that even paying for the little silver trinket and some card, a greetings card as special as this could be sold at a price that would give a decent profit for anyone who would make it.

But not me – it was exactly the kind of handcraft I would be terrible at. The filigree trinket would need to be sewn onto the card, and my stitching came in erratic jerks. I spoke to my friend Cindy about the idea and we agreed it could offer a way to promote Faik's business and a way for someone else to make money with the greetings card production. We just had to find a person who knew how to sew and showed some initiative to be willing to trial our idea.

Cindy and I talked about it as we made our weekly commute to one of Kosovo's most charming buildings – a *kulla* stone house near the 'Accursed' Mountains in the west of the country. It had been built a hundred years before in a vernacular architectural style that could be seen only in Kosovo and northern Albania, constructed in order to be defensible for families living in blood feud. Once a typical sight, the houses were disproportionately attacked in the conflicts of the 1990s and now few examples remained. This house was now running as a bed and breakfast offering seminar facilities, and Cindy and I had gone there for a break together with our partners. We'd eaten dinner by candlelight in the 'oda' men's meeting room which took up the top floor, where the mattresses and hand-embroidered cushions placed round the edge of the room offered perfect lolling opportunities and the woodstove made us all sleepy, and we became sleepier still with the *raki* firewater we shared round in espresso cups because we'd not found anything else to drink it from.

Now we were trying to share this *hygge* little corner of Kosovo with others, organising a series of six workshops to showcase the *kulla* and inviting the media to celebrate it with us. It was another part of Kosovo's cultural heritage though the mud of the village between the traditional high stone walls protecting each property couldn't have seemed further from the fine tweezer-work with precious metals of the filigree co-operative and my necklace. I certainly wasn't expecting these worlds to come together, but it was when we were inching through the mud that we met eighteen year-old Syzana.

She lived near the *kulla* and was curious to know what two obviously foreign women were doing in her small village. She came to introduce herself and we explained who we were and where we were from. We told her that we would have more foreigners coming at on Saturday and that we wanted to use the weekend to show off all that the village had to offer.

Syzana shrugged as if she couldn't believe that her village had much to offer, and then invited us round to dinner at her home, immediately offering us another example of what we wanted to share.

We were welcomed at her front door with a faint flicker of light.

'Power cut,' she shrugged again, steering us in the darkness over the step and through the difficulties of removing our shoes blind.

The subdued lighting hid at first the conditions that Syzana and her five brothers and sisters lived in with their parents – human relations were reduced to the warmth of voices, the feel of welcoming hands and offers of food and drink. Children giggled in the background but they darted beyond the feeble gleam of the improvised light held by Syzana's mother. Like a tired Vestal she held a saucer filled with vegetable oil from which trailed short cotton threads that had been lighted to work as meagre wicks.

Somehow in these conditions, and sheltered only in what I later saw was a portakabin made from plasterboard and donated by a Japanese aid agency after the war, Syzana's mother had brought up a brood of bonnie and bouncing children. The Albanian term of approval for a healthy child, *si rrush* – 'like a grape' – came to my mind as I looked at this bunch bobbing in and out of the dappling light. With a similar set of skills she had also managed to produce a large nettle *pite* pie and we feasted until I felt as round as a grape myself.

After the food her mother nudged Syzana. 'Show them, show them!'

It was the madam role traditionally adopted by mothers for their daughters' trousseau and Syzana looked appropriately embarrassed. But eventually she brought down a suitcase and opened it up to show the handiwork her mother had been wanting to boast of. There were table mats and coffee cup holders; knitting and crochet and lacy work called *oja*. Cindy and I looked at one another; we had found someone who certainly knew how to sew.

'You could sell these to the visitors who come to this weekend's workshop,' we urged her. She shrugged a third time as if she hadn't heard the suggestion or its implied praise, but when Cindy and I went to leave she bundled into little plastic bags some d'oyleys for each of us. I hoped it meant she'd understood that her crochet could have a value in the free market, not just the marriage market.

On Saturday I had hostess anxiety. I watched from the small windows of the *kulla* for LandRovers to nose through the large gates – would all the people who'd paid for the workshop manage to come? Would the journalists make it? Would the villagers seize the opportunity to sell their honey or their handcrafts?

The LandRovers arrived. TV crews and a documentary maker, and a curious group of expats. I could tell from the way their camera lenses engorged that they loved the building as much as I did.

But there was no-one offering things for sale from the village. The confidence that had had Syzana stopping two foreign ladies in the street when she'd struck up a conversation with Cindy and me had obviously deserted her now.

But this was just the beginning – there would be another workshop next week, and once the visitors left on Sunday Cindy and I went round the village again trying to explain.

No, we'd make no money from it. Yes, they could decide their own prices. No, there was no trick. Yes, we thought there would be a lot of interest and sales…

The next Saturday was a wine- and *raki*-tasting. We set out the glasses and bottles, my ears straining again for the sound of the gate, and evidence that someone was coming to embrace capitalism.

There was a sound and I started. Someone really was coming. The guy who'd offered cheese? Perhaps the brother who'd had some strange-shaped gourds he assured me people could buy as dippers 'to use for washing'?

It was Syzana, shyly rustling a plastic bag. She showed me what she'd brought – mats carefully beaded and crocheted by her and others in the family. When the guests arrived for the workshop we made sure that all of Syzana's neat products were sold.

The next week she came back with more, and with friends – the homemade cheese; cornflour ground in the village; a bag of walnuts. Our instinct about Syzana had been right – this was a young woman who knew about seizing opportunities.

So Cindy and I took Syzana out to coffee and asked her if she'd like to be a partner in the filigree greetings cards initiative. All the income from the project would go to her and we would make the initial investment in silver; after that she would have to keep back from her profits enough to buy the next batch.

We suggested we would start with buying 100 trinkets from Faik's co-operative. Together with Syzana we went shopping in Prishtina to buy the coloured card they would be sewn onto. She had the idea that the cards should be protected in cellophane 'you know, like with a woman's trousseau,' and when we showed that we didn't know and certainly had no idea where you'd get such stuff, she took us to the section of the market which specialised in preparations for weddings. The stalls here frothed with *mindila* – the lace-and-tulle handkerchiefs shimmering with glitzy gold or silver trim and traditionally held by a bride as she received guests or danced. Here you could buy sugared almonds, and the small fluffy hand towels with metallic thread decorating their edges which were wrapped in cellophane and given to wedding guests to put – inexplicably – under the windscreen wipers of their cars when they formed part of the wedding procession.

It was here also that you could buy the distinctive large sheets of sugar paper on which brides' handiwork was pinned like butterflies for display to her groom's family and guests. I'd been taken to such a public exhibition only once, visiting a friend's house before her brother's wedding. I'd been taken up to the room in her parents' house which would belong to the happy couple when they were married. The bed was covered with a new satiny quilt, with the tags still on it, and the headboard's virginity was guaranteed by it still being wrapped in plastic. Around the walls, the wardrobe, the mirrors and on every inch of space sheets of blue sugar paper had been hung with the bride's crafts on display. An embroidered apron, knitted socks, beadwork, crochet, and many – many – table mats. I didn't think that any family in Kosovo still invited guests to inspect the bed sheets the morning after a wedding, but the implications of this ritual had felt similar – I was being invited to appraise and approve the suitability of this new bride for the family, on the basis of the contribution she could make to the home economy, and in the hope that the care and neatness with which she stitched might reveal something about the way her DNA might knit with that of this home, and other produce she might be capable of.

Like the headboard, these precious symbols of virtue, obedience, hard work and nifty fingers had been sealed off in plastic, with each d'oyley on its backing paper covered with cellophane. So the market sold rolls and rolls of cellophane as one of the essential ingredients for a successful wedding. Syzana explained how you sealed the cellophane around the card by ironing it on and Cindy and I caught each other's eye again. We'd found the right collaborator.

It was a matter of days before the first hundred cards were available for sale, with Faik's intricate silver designs sewn carefully by Syzana onto a rainbow of cards, each accompanied by an envelope and presented in cellophane ironed tight. We sent out an email to our friends offering them for sale.

Within three days we'd received orders for a thousand cards. Faik's and Syzana's smiles rivaled one another for the pride they took in the project. Syzana got invited on national television to talk about the initiative and was asked to come and sell the cards at a prestigious gala night at Prishtina's smartest hotel. I offered to buy her a dress to wear that evening but she proudly told me she'd agreed with her parents that she could have money from what she'd earned from the cards to be able to buy one herself. She turned up looking gorgeous – shining like the luxury greetings cards which emerged from her cramped family home in the mud of the village. Once again I got the sense of how silver could shape people's lives, twisting and zigzagging into surprising new designs.

The reward for me came in having to make more frequent visits to visit Faik and his colleagues as we discussed designs for the cards and I collected orders. We were getting to know one another, becoming comfortable. They knew now that I didn't drink coffee, and offered me chamomile tea whenever I came to visit. Nor did we have to make conversation – I could just sit quietly and watch their work, learning the reality of the eye-strain and finger cramp which produced such beautiful objects.

I identified eight basic components from which all the pieces were made up. Most of them were based on threads – the 'filum' from which *fili*gree gets its name. But they also, more sparingly, used the other etymological component – 'granum', the grains or little balls added for decorative effect, as well as occasional little flat lozenges laid atop a lacy network of decorative wires. Of the techniques using the threads it was the 'mouse tooth' that most fascinated me. It was made using a tool with two small nails protruding. The silver thread was looped over one and under the other and with a deft twist of the wrist forward and backward it was shaped into a serpentine. The tool was then shifted further along the wire for another flick back and forward. Fatime's fingers at

Mouse teeth and the new directions silver can take   75

work on it moved as fast as someone knitting. At last after watching her produce a neat length of rodent incisors I asked tentatively, could I have a go myself. She smiled indulgently and ever so slightly smugly, and handed me the tool and the wire.

I knew exactly what to do, having watched her closely for so many hours. I held the wire and the tool just as she had done, and I flicked my wrist just as she did. Looking down at the wire I saw a slight irregular kink in it. Carefully I relooped it over and under the two nails and flicked my wrist back and forward just like Fatime. There was another kink in the wire now but instead of backing onto the first it was about a centimetre away. She helped me reposition the materials and held my wrist this time to show me how exactly I needed to jerk it. With her help the next manoeuvre was a little more successful. I took a sip of tea and tried again. Once again it failed. It was like a child sitting down at a piano having watched a professional in action. The hand movements seemed the same but the result was a discordant, messy disaster.

Fatime had been right to be smug – I would never get this.

'Oh, you will,' she assured me. 'But it might take seven or eight months.'

Silently I handed back the damaged silver wire and the stupid fiddly tool.

That day before leaving the workshop I bought a simple ring for myself. It was made up entirely of mouse-tooth, edged with a twist and a simple band. I wore it as a reminder against inappropriate ambition – in recognition of my limitations, and in gratitude for the skills of others.

Chapter 7. Brought to life at the Ethnological Museum in Prishtina

Everyone has an attic. It may not be under the eaves of a house but we all have a place where we keep our history. We often can't even articulate why we keep things that are no longer useful and may not be beautiful.

Countries need attics too, in the form of their national museums. Kosovo's was not behind Corinthian columns but through the high wooden gates of what is probably the oldest secular building in the capital. Originally the home of the Emin Xhiku family, the eighteenth and nineteenth century buildings of the Ethnological Museum glow like a jewel in Prishtina's dust and concrete. They glow with the emerald of the gardens, the amber of the carved and polished woodwork, and with the distinctive ruby red of handmade carpets and cushions.

Did they also glow with the silver or gold of filigree? This was my chance for the links in the chain of my necklace to connect me not only to the unexpected people and places I'd been taken to so far, but also to the crafts traditions in which it was born and worn.

I asked my guide at the museum, Bekim, whether they had filigree in their collection but he was evasive. First he took me round the older of the museum's buildings, which had been left as an eighteenth century city home would have been. We started in the 'room of fire' – a stone kitchen furnished with simple wooden furniture. I wondered whether I might enjoy spending time in my kitchen more if I were henceforth to refer to it as my Room of Fire.

To one side stood a waist-high wooden object of the dimensions of a chest freezer. One half of the lid was open while the other half was closed to create a horizontal surface. Bekim explained the practical and symbolic significance of the piece of furniture which was called a 'magje'. It was the storage bin for the family's flour, and the work surface where dough was kneaded, but it was also the source of status for women in the house. There would typically have been many women because of the Albanian tradition, still followed in many rural and even in some urban homes, of brothers bringing their wives back to their parents' home to live. All the women took turns at being given the key to the *magje* and being 'magjetore' for the day when they'd be responsible for cooking the bread for the whole family.

The importance of the *magje* was underlined by its carving and decoration. Bekim pointed out what I'd thought was a circular singe mark but which was probably, as he said, a sun. Elsewhere he pointed out the other sacred Albanian, and originally Illyrian, spiral symbol of the snake. Every home was said to have a protector house-snake which lived under the threshold. As a result Albanians would be careful about killing snakes in case they were unwittingly killing their protector. I'd heard an Albanian friend muttering to a snake that crossed our path when we were hiking in the hills here and Bekim explained that my friend would have been saying 'go away snake' three times. A real house snake would take that hint. If the snake remained then it wasn't your house snake so you could kill it with impunity.

From the basics of fire, stone, flour and snakes, climbing the stairs felt like moving forward through civilization. The upper storey held an elegantly proportioned room with elaborate carved wood along one wall and a raised seating area around a sophisticated copper brazier. Bekim pointed out how the room was set out in the interests of guests. It had two staircases leading to it – one from the kitchen, to be used by the family, and one from outside so that guests could come and go easily.

'In Albanian traditional law they say that "your home belongs to God and the guest".' I thought of Syzana's mother and her generous slices of nettle pie. Bekim went on, 'and no Albanian would turn away a guest if they needed a place to stay, even if they were a complete stranger.' He opened the carved wooden units set into the wall. 'These were filled with bedlinen so there would always be something ready for a tired traveller.'

We made our way down the guest staircase and into the shade of the shapely walnut tree in the garden. Now Bekim led me to the larger house, built by the family a hundred years later than the first building. This was the museum proper with exhibits supplementing the city house we'd just visited.

First he took me to the room set out like an *oda* meeting room in a *kulla*. I told him it was almost a replica of the room in the village where Cindy and I had run our workshops, where we'd got woozy on *raki* and woodburners; where we'd sold Syzana's crochet.

'You shouldn't have been there,' Bekim said with a smile. 'The *oda* was reserved only for men and even boys weren't allowed in until they were old enough to use a gun.'

But it didn't seem like he held it against me, and from there he took me on life's journey, through the imaginative curation of the museum.

We started in the 'room of birth' which was laid out to show the traditions of childbirth, including a pair of her husband's trousers left out for the woman to step over during her labour, to ensure her child was a boy.

From there we passed to the room of marriage and a dazzle of costumes. There was the sequined bling of the costume of the Gorani people centred near Prizren, the demure black and white of Dukagjini, the region where 'our' *kulla* was. But I wanted to see what would have hung at the plastic fingers and ears of the mannequins; I wasn't looking at the costumes.

I turned again to Bekim, 'But do you have any filigree?'

Instead of answering he turned away from me, to face the carved wooden doors of an antique built-in storage area. With a flourish he flung them open and I saw that inside, and lit dramatically against a black background, was a display of filigree jewellery.

It was breathtaking. Much was familiar from the work at
Faik's workshop, but there were also pieces that showed me
what that work could be transformed into with finer material.
The museum also has a library of books about filigree and
I feasted my eyes on more pieces collected in one building
than I had probably seen in all my travels this far. A gold
brooch used the double-headed eagle of the Albanian flag.
Red jewels were set in place of the eyes which gave it a
devilish look, with intensity increased by a larger red jewel
set where the heart would be. It could be the pulsating core
of Albanian nationalism, or the generous hospitality of this
culture – whose byword was 'bread, salt and our hearts'. Such
hospitality had in the course of this quest taken me in for
foraged pie even in its humblest homes, it had taken me out to
lunch in Mitrovica and good-naturedly fulfilled my strangest
whims, whether of going down a mine or to an overgrown
golf course. But as I stared at this exquisite bird I realised that
the red eruption from its breast could also be a wound; Bekim

Brought to life at the Ethnological Museum in Prishtina   81

reminded me that at various times in Albanians' history it had been illegal even to display the double-headed symbol of ethnic pride. There had been many occasions in the lifetime of this bird that it had borne a wound in its chest.

But leaving aside the symbolism, and focusing on the metalwork I admired the way that the techniques had been combined – 'granum' studs surrounding the heart jewel, interspersed with lozenges which gave an additional sense of the radiating intensity of that inset ruby. From there the gold wire scribbled airily and playfully – light enough that you could believe this creature really could become air-borne – until the feathered edges which were ended each with a distended spiral and a diamond tip. I noticed again the spirals which were such a feature of all the filigree I'd seen and Bekim reminded me of that sacred Illyrian symbol being worked into the very fabric of the jewellery.

There were more items displayed – cigarette holders where the granum studs were used in designs that could have been punk if they were smoked by the right people. Elsewhere pendants and brooches bloomed against the backing material. There were belts and buttons too – the latter substantial hollow barrels over an inch long and tipped with a cone. There was a triangular amulet as well. Bekim explained that triangles were always used to see off the evil eye, and that this one was typical in being hollow with a sliding opening to an internal compartment where a holy text could be inserted. There was something about being able to open the amulet that took it – literally – into another dimension; an interactivity that somehow brought it to life. I itched to try it, remembering how I'd hankered as a child after the toy cars that had doors that actually opened.

Bekim turned me back to the wedding costumes. He told me that his family were jewellers by tradition, having worked in Mitrovica. He had the jeweller's sense for metalwork as lived and used artefacts – 'These brides would have worn as much of the jewellery as they could have afforded. So you have to see this cupboard in combination with what's being worn by the models in these rooms. And think about the brazier we saw in the old house. Imagine that room filled with old rich men smoking their cigarettes from these holders.' It was the best kind of curation; not only for the objects and the rooms in this museum, but a curation of Kosovan culture; a reminder that things only existed within people's lives. Silver had been a part of the daily routines of the people who'd lived in these houses; it was a part of so many people's realities – from the Trepça miners to the charcoal burners of Brus, the filigree artists of Prizren and now the young entrepreneur Syzana. It had taken me a trip to a museum to properly understand the world outside the museum.

Brought to life at the Ethnological Museum in Prishtina   83

The next time I went to Faik's workshop I had a new understanding of the silver threads that had produced my necklace. They didn't just loop round into themselves, as I'd first seen that wire circling like some arcane Illyrian symbol around Faik and back into the extruding machine from which it came. I was learning that instead they were connections outward – into Kosovo's history and culture.

I had gone to the workshop to pick up another plastic bag full of the silver trinkets Syzana would sew on the cards. Faik greeted me this time with an odd formality. 'Mrs Elizabeth,' he said, 'we have something for you.' He picked up a small package sitting on the table. 'It's to thank you for helping to promote filigree,' and he handed it to me.

I unwrapped the plastic bag, murmuring thanks to Faik for his kindness before I'd even seen what he had given me. Inside sat an amulet. It was a triangle so I knew immediately it would see off the evil eye. Remembering what Bekim had taught me

I ran a finger nervously along one edge. Yes! Like the toy car whose doors really opened, it was one of the amulets with a sliding panel.

I didn't have a god whose sacred text I could insert there, but the next time I saw little Adena I asked her to write me something.

The piece of paper she wrote on fitted neatly into my charm and though her lettering was still uncertain, that made it all the more a source of faith, hope and love.

Chapter 8. Istanbul; the wellspring and the oxbow lake

Triangular amulets are an Islamic tradition, so the history of this object harked back to where Kosovo's Islamicisation had come from – the same place that Faik's language had come from, and his old postcard on the wall. It may be that filigree itself had come to Kosovo along Ottoman routes; it seemed that if I wanted to follow this thread back to its source I should go to the capital of the old Ottoman Empire.

My journey from Prishtina to Istanbul gave me a new lens to see both countries in. I hadn't noticed before just how much Turkish influence there was even in modern Kosovo. I had forgotten that the airport I would fly from was itself Turkish-owned and as I browsed the shops there I noticed the Turkish concessions and the Turkish imports even in Kosovan outlets.

Once on the Turkish Airlines plane more connections became evident. In front of me was a notice in English and Turkish: *Life vest under your seat*. In Turkish the word for the life vest was what I'd learned as an Albanian word for silver embroidered waistcoats – 'jelek'. I wondered what else I'd thought of as Albanian might turn out to have its roots elsewhere.

City, one-way street, neighbour, eyelash, waist, chain, link, shop, rent, customer, goods, bill, stamp, trick, good deed, fool, obstinacy, pleasure, socks, slippers, armchair, handbag, bell, cotton, copper, ribbon, sapling, pier, medicine, almond, aubergine.

This was the list I'd made by the end of my weekend in Istanbul. All familiar words I'd learned as Albanian which I saw in Turkish-language adverts, price lists and menus here and checked in my dictionary. The words are not the shared vocabulary of two languages which have borrowed and bred together, not the *three, trois, tre* exchanges of Indo-European cousins with two-way debts. This vocabulary read like a trader's catalogue; a guide to fine living brought by the Sultan's men to the mud and stone homes of fifteenth century Albania. Indeed, the concrete nouns share some similarities with a list I'd read once of what the pilgrims took to America on the Mayflower. It's a directory of civilising influences; a recipe for successful colonisation.

By the time we had landed at Istanbul's Ataturk Airport my mind was well back in that time before Ataturk, trying to imagine the Ottoman city and to sense where its silver craftsmen might be found. My first stop was going to be the Arasta Bazaar where I'd been told there was silver jewellery on sale.

But first I had to find it. At the airport I learned I didn't have the right visa. I got one in the end but I had to pay an extra administrative fee. Once through the airport and having failed to make a successful purchase in various shops I found out that the Turkish lire I had brought with me, given by a friend from a previous trip, wouldn't be accepted. It was a guy in Burger King who finally tried to explain, using Google Translate to hold up a message on his phone screen. 'Hello. Your money is old Turkish money. It will not pass here.' Having to communicate like this made me feel like I was deaf. I was certainly profoundly disabled.

And I was still nowhere near the Arasta Bazaar. I despaired of getting to see the silver jewellery I had come to find, and I fumed at my incapacity. This is not how I'd wanted my entry to the Ottoman capital to be; this was not how I'd wanted to experience traditional Istanbul.

But imagining this city – this Burger King – five centuries ago I realised that unwittingly I was in fact experiencing traditional Istanbul. Istanbul has always been a city of foreigners, with or without Google Translate. The history book I was reading while I travelled told me that 56 per cent of the Istanbul population in 1900 was non-Muslim. Istanbul is an entrepot, a trading centre, and foreigners and tourists have been part of its traditions for millennia. For centuries Istanbul has been a place where people don't know their way around the streets or the visa system.

Once I yielded to this comforting thought I stopped trying to be competent here, and instead opened my senses to spotting the heritage of Faik's silverwork in Prizren; the heritage of my necklace. From the shuttlebus into town I noticed flowerbeds along the motorway in the forms of stylised geometric flowers with low box hedges infilled with flowers. Along the Bosphorus, I glimpsed silver as fishermen flashed their lines, their buckets shimmering with bait behind them.

And at last I was in Sultanahmet, with the Blue Mosque and Ayasofya facing one another across a square. The older mosque was squat as a sumo wrestler, with the same flesh tones, and seemed coarse in contrast with the Blue Mosque's delicate minarets. But I remembered it from that cheaply reproduced photograph stuck in Faik's workshop, and I knew which wrestler I'd put my money on for staying power and sheer bulk and impact.

The Arasta Bazaar was nearby. It was quiet, ticking gently with the irregular clicks of dice and backgammon pieces in a café at the entrance.

A tout caught me and demanded, 'Where you from?'

'England,' I said, trying to make it easy for him, and for myself, and he told me about his family's shop and I assured him I didn't want a carpet.

'Many people from London but now with all this terror …' He spoke about it like the British complain about rain. But I could see for myself – the gunman who'd killed dozens of people celebrating New Year in an Istanbul nightclub in January had killed more than that.

With no crush of tourists it was easy to see into the shops along the market and I caught the glitter in some windows and headed to these.

Entering the first one there was a tinkle of a bell like the old-fashioned draper shops in London. The room seemed to shimmer and looking round I realised that there was in fact no bell but just a jangle of necklaces strung along the window with more hung at the wall. The slight breeze of my entrance had set them all jingling.

The owner got up from his glass of tea, his face a mixture of surprise and pleasure at having a customer.

I asked him whether he had any filigree and he assured me yes, yes.

'Is it handmade?' I asked.

Yes, yes, yes.

He brought out a tray of silver rings and I looked at them carefully. I had a new eye now, looking for the techniques I'd seen Bashkim and Fatime working. But there was no evidence of the hand-crafting I'd grown used to in their workshop. Although the designs were similar in their laciness I could tell now that they had been stamped out of pieces of metal.

'But these are machine-made,' I said.

Well yes, yes.

The owner brought out a tray of necklaces but looking at them I could see they were in the same style.

'Is there anyone who has *handmade* filigree?' I asked and he shrugged.

'Maybe the guy further down the bazaar?' he suggested so I tried there too, finding it again from the iron pyrites gleam of its window. But it was false gold indeed – the trays were the same machine work. I remembered Edith Durham's description of the shopping in Kosovo that nearly 'ruined' her. There she used the Ottoman terms 'alla turka' and 'alla franga' for 'Turkish-style' and 'French (foreign)-style'. She said 'It is a grand bazaar. Worth all the journey, for as yet it is but little spoiled with *alla franga*. The demand for very fine work is now slight – *alla franga* will maybe soon kill it.' And here I was a century later in the heart of the Turka and there was nothing but Franga.

I tried a further shop, once again crowded with gewgaws. As I turned to close the door behind me on my way in, my bag caught a display stand and tangled in some necklaces which were hanging there. I froze, suddenly remembering the Albanian song, 'The Potter' which I seemed on the verge of reenacting. It tells an unlikely sentimental story of an Albanian in the Istanbul bazaar, who breaks a vase in a shop and swears in Albanian at what he's done, only to be embraced by the potter, 'with two tears in his eyes', begging 'swear at me again like that' because he hadn't heard the words for such a time and longed to be reminded of his Albanian roots once more. I dropped an Albanian expletive at the necklaces I'd swept up with me and waited for a response. Nothing.

But at least the shopkeeper wasn't swearing back in any language. I apologised for my clumsiness and then asked him as I'd asked the others - 'Is there anyone who does handmade filigree in Istanbul?' He, too, shook his head sadly.

'You could try the Grand Bazaar though. There's a guy there called Zeki Tamirci who might be able to help.'

So I set off for the Grand Bazaar though with some skepticism. I'd started Turkish lessons and Zeki, Tamir and –ci were all words I knew – the name I'd been given meant 'Intelligent Fixing-man'. It sounded like it was made up.

There are over four thousand shops in the Grand Bazaar and I had no way of knowing which was Intelligent Fixing-man's but I started by asking. My first stop was at one of the spice stalls where I saw an opportunity. I'd heard that turmeric was good for memory and it seemed an appropriate thing to buy here, in a city teeming with memories I was trying to uncover. The owner of the stall gave me a delicious chocolate-covered pistachio with my change.

So he was friendly, and I asked whether he'd heard of Intelligent Fixing-man. Nope. But he could tell me the way to the jewellery quarter of the market where I should find him.

Following his directions I shouldered my way through the shoppers. There were more here than at the Arasta, but there was still an atmosphere of wary emptiness. On the wall hung a black ribbon with the slogan 'we won't give in to terrorism'. If the bazaar had been full with shoppers you wouldn't have been able to read it.

In among the shoppers were the delivery guys carrying tea and coffee on the distinctive trays fitted with an elegant metal superstructure from which they could be suspended. Burger King may have come to Istanbul but people here know that drinks taste better when they're not drunk from a sip-thru.

Once I was in the jewellery quarter it began to feel less of a wild goose chase. The first shop I tried here had heard of Zeki and the second was able to direct me. And soon I was in a small shop and jostling with the crowd at a high counter. Behind it was a table with men working over small pieces of silver, and my heart leapt. But squinting to make out what exactly they were working on I could see that this couldn't be filigree; the tools were too large. In comparison to the tiny tweezers used by Fatime and Bashkim the mallets and pliers seemed gross. And instead of the drama of the breath-regulated flame one of the men was using a space-age precision tool emitting a greenish flame.

Some things were the same here as in Prizren though. The same bell-shaped teaglasses next to the work, and a sprinkling of the fairy dust that always made the table in Prizren shimmer. But no rabbit leg.

Some of the men were engraving. A sign on the wall explained rhodium plating. Next to it hung a hieroglyphic alphabet and a pizza menu. There was beautiful comedic potential in a mix-up and someone getting *quattro formaggi* engraved on their bracelet.

The man at the counter was taking in completed pieces of jewellery and taking instructions from customers or jewellers, for the adjustment of rings or the decoration to be added. The jewellery was then put in one of a set of small old wooden boxes. Sometimes it was passed to the workers at the table but often it was hitched to a pole and lifted up. Following the pole with my eyes I saw there was a mezzanine level where at least one more man was working under an ancient arched ceiling gummy with pictures of basketball stars.

When it came to my turn at the counter I was asked what I wanted. I needed to enquire again whether they had handmade filigree but instead I found that the first question that came out of my mouth was whether Zeki Tamirci was the real name of a person.

It didn't go down well. The man I was talking to was apparently Mr Intelligent Fixer-man himself and yes, he assured me, it was his real name. Could I please in exchange for his answer tell him what I wanted.

Well, did they have any handmade filigree?

No, they didn't.

Was there anyone in the bazaar who made filigree by hand?

No, there wasn't.

Oh.

'Well, thank you very much.'

'There's Yusuf of course,' someone reminded Mr Intelligent-but-quite-grumpy Fixing-man.

'Ah yes, there's Yusuf…'

So I was directed once again to a bewildering address in the bazaar, and eventually I found him.

Yusuf Erin was in his sixties. He came to Istanbul in 1961 but had been born and raised in the city of Mardin less than twenty miles from the Syrian border. Now he spends his days in a small space within the bazaar, hung round with jewellery. The pendants looped across the walls are displayed like some men would show off their medals; these are Yusuf's badges of achievement.

But he explained that even he no longer makes filigree. Seeing my face fall he hurried to tell me that he had once – when he was in Mardin, where his was one of thirty filigree-worker families, the others mostly Assyrian Christians. He guessed that there might be four still there now.

He got out the Mardin work to show me and the pieces took my breath away. They were beautiful, yes, but what gave me prickles along the back of my neck – right into the clasp of my necklace – was that they were beautiful in exactly the same way as Faik's pieces were beautiful. Mardin is 2400 kilometres from Prizren, almost exactly the distance from London to Prizren. And yet the craftspeople working on these earrings, necklaces, rings, bracelets and belts were coiling wire, forming flowers, and spiraling their way through them – in precisely the same way as the Prizren co-operative. I'd been a fool to think that globalisation meant Burger King.

There were amulets with a space for written prayers or holy script, like mine from Faik, and one bracelet was made up of double-decker flowers just like those that Faik and Mr Pasule had shown me. A slim curved spindle-shaped brooch was particularly fine. It was made up of two paisley leaves infilled with spirals and surrounded with zigzags over which four *petit pois* 'granum' balls had been fixed. I'd love to watch these being made ….

Could I go to Mardin, I asked Yusuf but he shook his head sadly. 'It's not safe because it's so close to the Syrian border. There's a nearby village, Midyat, where there are another ten families who do this work, but that's too close to the war in Syria too.'

Second best was buying the brooch so I gave Yusuf the money for it. He wished me the standard blessing for new clothes or adornment, *iyi günlerde kullanın* 'may you enjoy it in good days.'

So was this where my hunt had ended for now? A metalwork technique which had originated somewhere in the Ottoman Empire, springing up in bright white wires like water from a source, and which had then flowed to Istanbul like all good ideas and fine things had done during the centuries of the Ottoman Empire's sway. And from Istanbul it had pooled with other ideas and techniques and spilled over, following the paths worn by soldiers and tax collectors out across the empire, to new land like Kosovo. But then the central pool had dried up, the paths become unnavigable as new barriers and borders were raised, and the other dribbles and puddles had, for whatever reason, dried up too. So was it really the case that Prizren existed like a cultural oxbow lake – an enchanting, shimmering reservoir of skill and beauty, but no longer connected either to Istanbul or to its own source, and thus threatened very soon to atrophy.

And out of the totality of skills that had flowed through these metallic currents all that was left was just a few Kosovars like Faik, Bashkim and Fatime and their colleagues in the small room of the former tobacco factory in Prizren, and – thousands of miles away – thirteen families in a war zone …

Never had the crafts from Prizren seemed so precious.

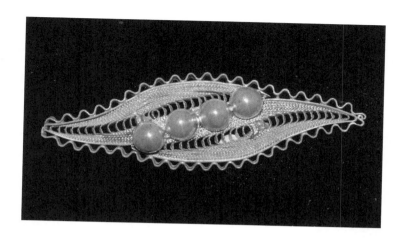

~ THE SILVER THREAD ~

Chapter 9. Inconspicuous consumption; jewellery-making in Communist Albania

Rob had a new job and I fretted that our move would take me away from the spools of silver that had helped me find my way round Kosovo and fall in love with it. However, his new office was only in Tirana, the capital of neighbouring Albania. 'There'll be silver workers there too,' he promised me.

One of his new colleagues soon heard about my interest and before I knew it the silver was working again like a shiny key to make connections with new people and help me understand a country. Ama invited me to the home of her in-laws one evening to talk to them about their decades of jewellery-making during Communism.

I stepped over the threshold into only the second Albanian home I'd been invited to in Tirana. But it didn't feel like truly new territory – after all, I had now visited many Albanian homes in Kosovo, from Feimja's guesthouse in Novo Brdo to Syzana's simple family prefab in Dranoc. Remembering the rules, I bent to take my shoes off at the door of the Oroshis' house.

Mrs Oroshi, Gjuzepina, stood inside the door and looked at me as I stooped.

'No, no; no, there's no need,' she said.

'Of course I will,' I insisted, fiddling with zips.

'No, no; please no,' she begged me and I looked up at her quizzically. She had a soft, kind face. It stared down at me and below it swung a small, fine silver cross from around her neck.

I realised that this was the first Christian Albanian home I had been to here. And the tradition of removing your shoes was a Muslim one … I mumbled an apology and obediently did the zips up again.

Gjuzepina was still smiling, unbothered by my embarrassment.

'Come in, come in,' she gestured me into the cosy warmth of her front room. Her husband stood behind her and greeted me.

'I didn't work in jewellery-making,' he said almost immediately. 'It was Pina who worked at the Artistike factory. I was in metal machining.'

I was surprised at this as I'd been told that both of them had produced jewellery, but of course it was no problem, and I turned to Pina.

'You need to ask her, not me. My work was in the factory that made much larger pieces,' repeated Françesku.

I assured him that I would be happy to talk just to his wife then, and when we'd all sat down I asked Pina to tell me about her work at the Artistike factory and what silver had made of her days and years during the Enver Hoxha regime.

Across the Tirana cityscape, factories like Artistike cast long shadows, like old sins. None of them are still functional yet they shape the geography of the city. If you stand at a central point in Tirana you can decide on whether to catch a bus to Porcelani – named for the old ceramics factory – or to 'Kombinat', named for the former Stalin Textile

Factory; both now shut, despite what the bus timetables offer. The community where I'd started volunteering for a reading project was in a suburb which I could direct taxi drivers to only by the landmark of the Enver Hoxha Tractor Factory. No matter that Enver Hoxha was dead and the factory closed, abandoned, blotched with damp and graffiti, ransacked for any reusable materials until only its useless concrete skeleton remained, with lumps of building material dangling dangerously from rusting rebars. For all Tirana's new apartment blocks, and the enthusiasm with which old buildings are razed with a lust for ever shinier new construction projects, it is still by means of the old monsters that the city is navigated.

But Pina's story of her time at Artistike was not the story of industrial decay I had prepared myself for. She spoke affectionately of her history and displayed on the low table in front of me a series of carefully made filigree platters, a vase, small items of jewellery, and a little box, along with an extremely intricate white silver cigarette holder made from wire which was truly as fine as human hair. I recognised designs from the Prizren workshop.

Now I'd crossed a border and was building a new life away from Kosovo I was struck even more by the continuity of traditions despite political boundaries; these crafts were a very real shared language between the craftspeople of Albania and its neighbour. Even when Albania had shut its borders in isolationist paranoia, and families here couldn't even communicate with relatives in Kosovo, Pina had been bent over her wire at Artistike spelling out meaning with exactly the same craft alphabet as had been used by Bashkim and Fatime in Prizren.

Looking at the delicate handcrafts it was even more incongruous to hear Pina's story of working conditions at 'Artistike'. She'd started there in 1966 at the age of sixteen, first with six months of unpaid training, and then over more than a decade progressed through the six 'kategorite' of employees to the top category where she continued for the rest of her labouring life. She described her work as part of a 'brigade' of twenty people and I imagined a little army of women (she said that the majority of the workers had been female) – the Filigree Brigade, perhaps armed with fine swords glittering with intricate details, with platters as shields, made impractical by the gaps in their lacy craftsmanship? I remembered the pincers and tweezers and the fire-blowers of Faik's group and imagined them advancing in regimented groups led by a brigadier hoisting aloft a carefully crafted twinkling red star.

Altogether, Pina had worked in her brigade for over thirty years, until the factory was privatised along with all state enterprises and then closed in 1997. She talked about the quotas they were given for production and the extra hours everyone had to work to make sure the quotas were met – on penalty of receiving no pay at all that month. She spoke without bitterness of how all their work went to export, and of the tiny wages she received. Instead of evoking the abandoned hulk of the Enver Hoxha Tractor Factory, her narrative reminded me of the paintings I'd seen in Tirana's National Gallery showing the noble labour of the factories – girls with bright eyes staring far into the future, workers' aprons whipped by unseen currents which might be the roar of furnaces or the wind of change; men with good cheekbones and women with practical biceps all moving together, moving forward together.

There had been 120 people employed in the factory. 'All dispersed now,' she commented, and it was a wonder – the idea of 120 front rooms across the city, like this one each with a woman or man quietly proud of the forgotten work of their nimble fingers.

'Do you do anything like it now?' I asked. But Pina said she didn't have the patience ... 'or the eyes.'

She moved her hands over the vase on the table as she spoke and I returned to looking at the designs. But not only some of the designs but also the metal was new to me, 'It's the first time I've seen copper filigree,' I said.

She shrugged, 'Silver is so expensive.'

On the other side of the room Françesku intervened, 'We got metal from wherever we could. This stuff was copper wire made for the electrical factory in Shkodra. For the things I made I'd use whatever people brought me.'

The things I made …

'So you did make jewellery yourself?' I queried, wondering how my Albanian was letting me down in the confusion I had about just what job Françesku had had during the regime. He looked uncomfortable.

'I couldn't work at the same factory as Pina – there was a rule that you couldn't have two people from the same family employed in one place. I did it … how do you say, Ama? *Illegally*, eh?'

I shrugged, in the same way Pina had just done when I commented on the copper. Honesty is so expensive.

'When times are hard in England I'm sure people do things illegally just to keep alive?' he pointed out and I rushed to agree.

'So what did you make?'

Bit by bit, Françesku explained how during Communist times people would bring him old hidden bits of silver or gold for him to rework into wedding rings for their sons or daughters. It was illegal because of a regime which didn't allow private business, or the holding of private property.

'It sounds dangerous,' I commented.

'It was,' he agreed, and told me about a neighbour who was a doctor and had therefore had more money than others living nearby. The doctor's wife had gone shopping with a string shopping bag. 'With that bag everyone could see the luxuries she was buying,' he said, 'and they gave her a warning, "don't go shopping with a string bag"'. I wasn't sure whether he was speaking metaphorically. Maybe he hadn't been sure either, in that strange topsy-turvy era of inconspicuous consumption where a metal trinket was a shameful secret.

I remembered what I'd read about the regime and how at its height one in three people had been a spy for the Sigurimi secret services. 'Did no-one ever find out?' I pushed.

'I had good friends,' said Françesku.

I thought he meant people in positions of authority, but as he went on I realised he meant people with more power even than that. 'One was a plumber, one was an electrician and one was a tailor. Through helping them with jewellery-making I could pay them back for the ways they helped me; we needed each other. It was the same with food – someone would get a piece of beef they'd sneaked down from the village, and someone else would have vegetables, and we put it all together.'

Again, despite the hardships and the fearful regime this couple were describing, in a land where your nuggets of meat and metal alike had to be hidden from the authorities, I caught a glimpse of nostalgia. On an impulse I asked, 'so are things better now?'

Françesku shook his head but then I remembered what an ambiguous sign this is in Albania where shaking usually means 'yes'. Perhaps he wasn't certain himself.

'It's not what we thought it would be,' he said eventually, and started telling his memories of the demonstrations which finally brought down Enver Hoxha's regime. 'A river of people! Democracy exploded,' he said, 'right here,' and I realised how close this house was to the university accommodation where the demonstrations had begun.

'So was it only after Democracy that you got these beautiful things?' I asked Pina, remembering what she'd said about all the production of the Communist factory going for export.

'I only got them when the factory closed,' she said. 'The employees asked the supervisors if we could make one or two objects each and keep them as souvenirs and they said it was OK. Some of the other things I bought in a shop more recently. They were made by a guy in Albania but he's gone to Italy now.'

I traced the familiar shapes, picking up a platter made in a style I recognised, with a large stylised flower of ten petals, each infilled with a distended spiral and two tight miniature coils, and then edged with zigzags and surrounded by a circlet from which more than forty further petals radiated out, each again filled with nine more delicate coils. On another platter about fifty paisley pairs sprouted from the second circle of petals, exuberantly forming a flower around a flower. These were then edged with double ram's horns, each infilled once again with a dozen small coils. The minuteness of the work and the sheer volume of it was breathtaking.

'This one is called "mouse tooth,"' I told Ama, as Faik had taught me, pointing knowledgeably to the looping zigzags which edged the vase. I told her the Turkish word for it – *siçan dish* – but Pina was frowning.

'We called it *bishti i miut*,' she said. It meant 'mouse tail' and looking at the way the silver wire was swept back on itself in a loop I had to admit that it looked more like a mouse's tail than a rodent's sharp tooth. I wondered whether there had been some dyslexic exchange between the Turkish 'tooth' *dish* and the *bisht* that meant Albanian 'tail'.

'But these are so small. We worked on much bigger things. My brigade made Skanderbeg on his horse, all in filigree.'

'Even the horse,' added Françesku, and I wondered where on earth Enver Hoxha's government had found an export market for filigree models of fifteenth century Albanian heroes on horseback.

He sighed, thinking of Skanderbeg and of past glories. 'We wanted to pass this tradition on to our children like Pina had it from her family,' and he told me about her uncles and his father and grandfather who had all been filigranists. 'We have no wealth to leave but at least the children could have a skill.'

Ama got out her smartphone to show me some photographs from her brother-in-law's Facebook page,

'The boys do pieces of metalwork'. She brought up pictures of small trinkets not of filigree but carefully cut out and inscribed – a family shield, name necklaces, a cross.

'It's not their main job,' said Françesku. 'They work in a bar which takes up most of their time, but they do this in their spare time.'

'Like you did under Hoxha?' I smiled. So nothing had changed with the coming of the free market except that people working the second job they needed to keep their family fed could do so without hiding the fact. And now instead of avoiding net bags Albanians sought out a different kind of net to show off their material wealth.

'But why are you interested in all this?' asked Françesku. 'I told Ama not to bring you here because we're not experts in all this – we're just simple workers. And you're asking us all this about our memories, not about the silver.'

I tried to explain, 'I'm interested in how silver links with people's lives …'

Françesku interrupted me. 'It wasn't living,' he said bluntly. 'We survived by a hair's breadth; you had to be very careful.'

He searched for how to express something. 'There was no flow to your life: you lived just drop by drop.'

As if this had reminded him of something, he reached for a bottle behind him. It was Hungarian Unicum bitters and he poured me a glass. With the rich herbal flow of an imported spirit we toasted one another, and Albania, and metalworkers – young and old, legal and illegal, Kosovar and Albanian. I thanked him for his family's warm hospitality, for their memories, for their frankness and all they'd taught me.

As I was leaving, Pina picked up one of the most fragile items she'd displayed on the table – the exquisite silver cigarette holder.

'It's for you,' she said simply, with the boldness and generosity of a family who'd risked imprisonment to make the rings for a friend's wedding. It sat in my hand as light as a leaf. I thanked her profoundly. I would never use it, but I would display it proudly, and perhaps she knew this – that what sometimes makes things precious is the chance to show them off.

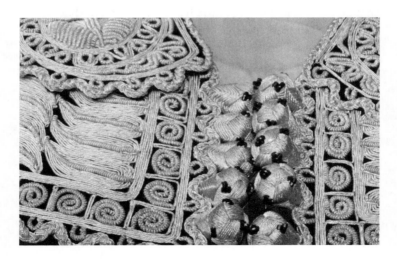

Chapter 10. Caring for Albania's silver trophies in Tirana

The 'Ambasador 2' is a smart address at a point which forms a tight equilateral triangle with Tirana's American Embassy and the Sheraton Hotel: the places that silver is spun. It's to this apartment block that Linda Spahiu had suggested that I came to meet her to see her collection of 'silver threads'. This would be my chance to see Albania's filigree and the motifs I'd first come across in my necklace but now in the broader context of handcrafts, and especially the weaving of silver within textiles. I'd been told that Linda had an 'atelier' so I imagined I would find there a chic dilettante in the traditional crafts of Albania. I guessed from her voice on the phone that she was in perhaps her fifties or sixties and I thought of elegant collectors and connoisseurs I'd met through NADFAS, the Arts Society, in the UK. She'd no doubt have beautiful accessories …

As arranged, I called her again when I arrived at the tower casting its welcome long shadow on this day of dazzling summer heat. She'd said she'd come to get me and I stood waiting at the entrance feeling unattractively damp and sticky from my walk across town, and not well prepared for ethnographic exchange.

From behind me I heard a quavering call, 'Mrs Elizabeth?'

I turned to find a woman with a towel round her shoulders coming towards me with a sweet smile and a hand outstretched. Slight panic because I didn't recognise this face, and I was aware that Linda would be down soon to meet me so I didn't want to get caught in conversation with someone who looked like she was in the middle of having a hair cut.

'I'm Doctor Linda,' she said and steered me by the shoulder away from the smart apartment block and round a corner to a warehouse emitting strains of tinny radio music.

It took me a while to navigate this double surprise – that I was being taken not to an apartment atelier at a smart address but to a garage round the corner from it, and that it was not hairdressing but simply the heat that had prompted the towel round the neck of the woman who was accompanying me. She was a practical woman – later she gestured at her white rubber sandals and reminded me that she had been a paediatric doctor for most of her professional life. She was also clearly a woman with an instinct for care, attentive to me but even more so to the creations – one might even call them creatures – with which she was surrounded. Once we were inside the workshop and into conversation she talked about her artefacts the way old women might discuss adopted cats – dear strays about whose presence in her life she was slightly exasperated, but to whom she was offering a home while she waited for the authorities to do their duty.

I had clearly interrupted her – a fine piece of damaged silk fabric was spread out on a table placed to catch the best of the light, with dangling needle and thread which must have been set aside when my phone call came. I asked about the restoration and how she learned to do this work but she frowned away the question – perhaps as if I'd asked how you learn to care for a cat. 'The objects tell you what to do – they have a voice. You smell them, you touch them with your fingers –' she used the Albanian word for fingerpads which translates as 'little apples'. 'And you ask people,' she went on

– 'our mothers, our grandmothers know how they used to look after these objects in their homes.'

She told me that she'd been doing conservation by instinct for years when she'd finally found a way to access some expertise to help her. Online she'd found a UNESCO manual from 1974, written in English for the benefit of conservationists working in Iraq. She doesn't speak English but with Google Translate she had been able to convert it into Italian, which, like most people in Albania, she is proficient in.

Patched together – like a piece of frayed silk – from Google Translate and online documents, her conservation regime is impressive. She told me that every item in her collection has a code and an invoice detailing its sale because, as she put it, 'Every object needs to have its own passport'. She'd compiled a photographic inventory and kept a copy in a safe; another copy had been sent to the mayor of Tirana – because, as she said, using an archaic Albanian formulation, he's the *zoti i shtëpisë* 'head of the household' where these items are preserved – and a third had been sent to the Ministry of Culture.

I looked at the splayed strands of the silk she was stood over, and thought about the fragility of objects – and people – washed up around the world. Around me was quite a range of flotsam that Linda had rescued. One wall was hung with a shower of distaffs. I'd seen these at the ethnological museum in Prishtina and I knew that traditionally they had been made by suitors or brothers as gifts for their womenfolk who would have needed them for spinning. Here they were mounted on the wall like the tools in my father's garage, each hung in their own space, their forks and arms and horns and points loosely tessellating. Off to one side was a wooden latticework window like I'd seen in the UNESCO World Heritage Site city of

Gjirokastër in southern Albania. But as Linda started moving around her space and opening drawers and cupboards it became evident that there was far more here. What I had taken to be curtains hung around the walls were pulled back to reveal deep drawers which Linda opened and from which she carried out packages which she unwrapped on the table for me. Looking up I saw that on one side of the room the curtains were double height, and soon Linda was making her way carefully up some steps and revealing further shelves and hanging spaces. I had thought we were in a room with some storage space around the edges; I realised we were in fact occupying a small empty space within a vast wardrobe.

'Er, how many objects do you have exactly?' I asked in wonder.

One thousand three hundred!

'How did you get to own so many?' I asked, and with an indulgent smile at her familiars Linda deftly turned around the question, which she must have been asked before. 'I don't own them; they own me.'

She went on to tell me how she had started funding her collection by selling her house and then the house that had been in the name of her teenage children. So this is what silver's threads could mean to your life if you let them. Gently I asked what the children thought about their mother's priorities.

'They tolerate me. They say, "we'll support you now, but after you – "' it was a tactful expression of mortality "' – we won't do what you do. It's depressing.'"

'And why…?' the question was obvious. Looking at the fine craftsmanship the answer might also have seemed obvious. I care about these things – but I wouldn't sell my children's home for them.

Linda didn't answer me directly. She was pulling out a shimmering piece of old textile and said in disbelief and a kind of revulsion, 'Do you know that people cut up these things to make *slippers*'. You could imagine she was talking about cats again. Their beauty and integrity speaks for itself but she added something else – 'people need to feel part of a process. And Albania has not yet been discovered … by Albanians. To see how my grandparents dressed I have to go online.'

Slowly the story came out of how she saw her role in this – starting with the just one or two items which she had brought out to show friends when they came to her house. Then people had started to bring others to see the items, to come 'on pilgrimage' as she described it, or to tell her of people who were selling up prior to emigrating, and getting rid of all the layers of their own history – the knots and threads and loops handed down father to son, and the trousseaus shuttled across looms by virgins and rattled in wedding chests on horseback across rough landscapes to their marital homes. It was her who was called when people were knocking down old houses containing architectural elements that could be salvaged.

I have a friend in England who works to rescue street dogs who've been impounded and are due to be euthanised. Linda's stories sounded similar – the calls at short notice, the rush around the country to reach the precious things before they were destroyed. It was even familiar to hear about the bargaining that Linda described – the family about to leave their house with its intricately carved wood ceiling to the wrecking ball who told her that if she didn't get there quickly they'd sell the carvings out of the country, into Montenegro. She'd been alerted to the destruction of homes of Albania's heroes: a house painted by Kolë Idromeno and the 270 year-old home of founding father Luigj Gurakuqi – one of my favourite frock-coated patriots (I am always a sucker for the first education ministers of new countries and Gurakuqi was also director of Albania's first teacher training college – a revolutionary through pedagogy).

Only occasionally, she said, do people donate the items. She told the story of a lad from an agricultural college who'd seen her on TV. He had had just two things passed down to him – two spectacular costumes inherited from his mother and his grandmother. He had come to Linda with a Sophie's Choice; she could take one and he would keep the other as a memento.

Linda gives such pieces refuge, but she's also found a modest way to preserve and promote them through small installations which incorporate the items; little vignettes or set pieces which can be displayed on a wall. The handwoven silk fabric, for example, was to be hung behind the lattice in a display which she says she wants to hint at the world of the feminine kept in separate areas of the traditional houses in Albania in the past. She showed me a photograph of another called 'Seven Men' which incorporated the traditionally showy men's waistcoats, an ornate holder for gunpowder, a gun – a homage to testosterone. Or perhaps a critique of it, as if it is in these items and only in these items that Albanian manhood resides. I asked Linda which it was but she just replied, 'Men aren't these men any more – that fire was fighting for independence. That's fine, but what's left today?' Gazing at the brash stripes of the old waistcoat fabric and the apparently murderous barrel of an empty revolver it seemed as good an image as any for the crisis of masculinity I'd heard diagnosed as one of modern Albania's main challenges.

This piece was now hanging in a private residence in Saudi Arabia and I couldn't tell whether she was proud or rather uncomfortable about that. I probed and she shrugged. 'It's preserved them. These installations give them a voice. And the money goes to enabling further work to preserve the artefacts.' The government does occasionally buy such items from her to give as diplomatic presents, and one of Tirana's largest hotels has a display in its glossy lobby. Businesses had started to buy them too 'where they used to hang a picture of a lake, a moon, and a boat' as Linda described it and I sensed her pride not just in sharing the past but also in a wider project of educating people's taste. And I felt she should be proud at this way for Albanians to make friends, by exchanging their stitching for diplomatic favours. Some of the women's costumes here were hung with old coins and it was fitting to think of these becoming international currency once again.

She had tried opening a museum to showcase her collection, but she had grown disillusioned at the absence of support from Albania's state institutions, and the government's lack of interest in doing anything to promote either her artefacts or the 33 000 items she said they have in the state archives. But she had established herself now as a small unofficial source of support – and hope. She mentioned the town of Kruja which is the centre of Albania's meagre antiques trade. 'Twenty years ago Kruja wasn't like it is now – the artefacts were left lying on the floor. But people from there came here to learn how to look after them.' Ironically such care of course only hastens the items' likely departure from Albania, snapped up by tourists who take them off to Saudi Arabia – or my own home in Cornwall. 'The items go on *gurbet*,' she acknowledged, using the untranslatable Albanian word that has something of migration and something of exile in it, and which has been the fate of so many - the persecuted, fortune-hunters, desperadoes, the impoverished or criminal from this country who have sailed out in a brave, bold diaspora for more than a century.

But some of the items were actually going home, I realised – Linda was pointing out to me the wool that came from England which was used for luxury embroidery in Albania. These items are as much on *gurbet* during their sojourn here as their sisters spun in Albanian mulberry trees which end up in foreign collections.

With this wealth of activity I was a little bewildered. 'So do you have a particular focus?' I asked, clutching at silver threads and finding intricate patterns unwinding as I did so.

'Yes,' Linda said simply. 'I'm focused on costume, but if you know how someone made their bed, how they laid their table, you understand the 'aquarium' in which the costumes were worn.

'And you're here for the silver embroidery, right?' she reminded me, in the midst of my bedazzlement. She started to show me how silver swam through her collection in the bright tropical 'fish' here. Some of the artefacts made an impact immediately with their bold, dramatic colours (Linda told me that Albanian traditional costumes use no half-tones), and others came to life under the careful curation and interpretation that Linda gave me. Asymmetry, for example, was something I'd not noticed as a consistent feature of traditional Albanian crafts.

One after another, she unwrapped from their ghoulish shrouds the people-sized, people-shaped relics. The wrapping in sheets was apparently the approved conservation practice but she joked, 'I don't have any bedlinen left in my house.' She was smiling but I imagined she might actually be telling the truth. A woman who would sell her home for the sake of her collection would probably think little of sleeping on a bare mattress. Or maybe, I mused, she slept here, keeping watch; keeping company.

There was a waistcoat crowded with flowers growing in a thicket of metallic thread. On another, hazelnut-sized silver knots, each topped with a glass bead, formed a double row of perhaps forty buttons, laid against thick silver braid in rows parallel with more silver stitched in twists, crocheted, and finally taking flight in whorls and spirals and acanthus wreaths. A pair of purple shoes was zigzagged in silver braid; a hand-woven silk shirt jangled with sequins attached to the delicate fabric with decorative silver thread; plum-coloured velvet had crewel-work shiny tulips, stars and moons. 'Silver was believed to see off the evil eye,' Linda explained about the over-representation of this particular material throughout the costumes she showed me.

The work was intricate, exhausting to think of. With one eye on my watch I considered each stitch in terms of seconds, each pattern in terms of hours; these were clothes but also diaries: the record of their days, their dreams, their lives, made by women who lived before photographs – or beyond photographs.

'And made by men,' corrected Linda. She said that the sewing of the toughest fabrics required physical strength and wasn't done by women. She got out a photograph from 1900 showing men at work on silver embroidery in the northern Albanian city of Shkodra.

As she took out each new item she announced it like a tour guide, 'and here we're in … Elbasan/ Gjakova/ Mirdita.' I felt like she really was travelling in time and space through these rich fabrics.

She also talked me through the movement of symbols first carved on stones in permanent places and that were then seen

carved in wood – in more portable items – and finally made their way into designs on clothing. 'About 300 years ago the same designs start to be seen on costume. Maybe people had started moving around more then, and their costume became their home.' It's true that a surprising amount of the silver lines stitched into the black cloth of an apron, for example, were straight, combined into ziggurats or darts that would have been a more natural design for a chisel to make than a needle.

With some effort, she levered out of a deep drawer a *xhubleta* and passed it to me to weigh in my arms. This traditional dense and heavy felt hooped dress can be up to sixteen kilograms and was worn by Albanian women in Kosovo, Albania and Montenegro and is thought to be related to a dress seen in Neolithic figures from Bosnia. She set it down and showed its rigidity, 'A *xhubleta* has to stand up on its own – without the woman in it. It's a memorial,' she said, and then took me on a tour of the garment's symbols, much as a

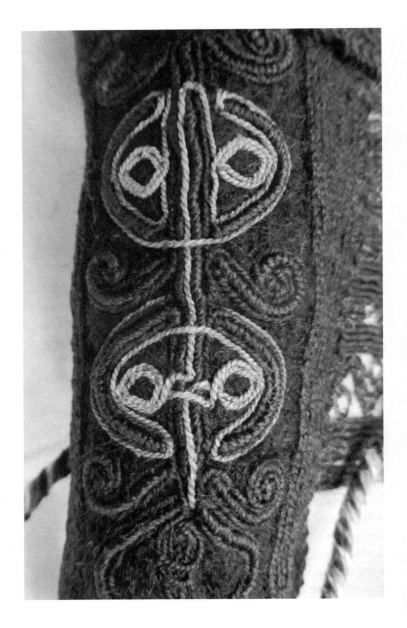

Baedeker guide might talk you through the inscriptions on a cenotaph.

'These are not forms of individual creativity,' she emphasised. 'If you ask any of the women who've worked on these about why they used a particular design they would answer "*kështu bëhet*" – "that's the way it's done."'

She'd like the *xhubleta* to get UNESCO World Heritage status and of course she was talking now about the item of clothing as a concept, not about any particular example of it. '*Xhubleta* is a book,' she said, 'and each individual one is a page but we need to collect them together if we want to read the narrative.'

The narrative they tell is a clear biography – Linda showed me the three *xhubletas* that even a poor woman would have had as a minimum (richer women could have had as many as ten). One was called the 'good *xhubleta*' – worn on her wedding day. Then there was the 'beyond the good *xhubleta*' she'd wear as a married woman. A third *xhubleta* was worn after the birth of a woman's first son. When she was buried she wore the 'good' one and Linda told me of talking to a woman in panic when she thought her good *xhubleta* was damaged. 'I need to wear that when they bury me,' she'd said, 'or my late husband won't recognise me.'

She wound the *xhubleta* up once again in their sheets. Were these body bags, protecting the remains of old soldiers who were abandoned behind enemy lines? Or did Linda's tenderness make this more like a bedtime parenting ritual, tucking the costumes up in her sheets and wishing them a safe night.

It was time to leave and I congratulated Linda on all she was doing. She looked mournful – a single ageing woman on a hot day. She was pink with the heat and although she had been wearing lipstick, all that was left now were the more resilient contours of lipliner. She looked as though she herself needed some restoration. 'I wanted to save things,' she said. 'But I realised I couldn't save everything.' I saw how she'd tried to work her way out of this obvious truth – the attempts at commercialisation, the attempts at awareness-raising. She'd saved so much and I wondered whether there was some frail hope for the craftsmanship and creativity we both cared about.

But when I stepped outside her workshop it was into the dust being kicked up by construction work on the nearby stadium costing the silver of fifty million euros. Albania had qualified that year for the European Championships for the first time, and UEFA had threatened to pull qualifying matches out of the country without a new stadium. As Linda had said, 'people need to feel part of a process,' and this was the process that Albanians were investing in today. It seemed that the roaring national pride of Albania aspired to shiny trophies on the international stage and not the aged silver finessed through women's handwork over generations.

Chapter 11. Queen of the *xhubleta*

I was feeling part of a process now: my necklace had been a link in a chain. It was not just a connection to Rob and his adventures in Kosovo, or even just to Kosovo; now I was learning new ways of understanding where I lived. One day, walking through the central Skanderbeg square in Tirana I took time to admire the striking socialist realist mosaic on the front of the National Museum. It shows a procession of Albanian heroes and heroines from throughout history – a meaty Illyrian warrior with sharp calf muscles, a soldier in white *fustanella*, a frock-coated intellectual from the nineteenth century, a beefy-armed woman with a stick, a factory worker in a leather apron. All were hastening forward – the intellectual as if he was late for a meeting, the Illyrian as if he was about to rip your heart out – and led by a woman. She's slight and wears impractical shoes but she inspires her motley crew forward with arms aloft, and in one of them she's brandishing a rifle. It's a glorious image but only now that I'd met Linda did I notice the dramatic dress of the woman heading towards us across the square. She was wearing a *xhubleta*, distinguishable from the felt bands around the bottom, and the undulations of the rim. The reason that I hadn't identified it as a *xhubleta* before was that it was almost entirely white. All the dresses I'd seen at Linda's atelier were black, with the occasional flashes of silver or gold in their motifs.

When I asked about the strange white skirt, my friend, the writer Flutura Açka, told me, 'if you want to know about *xhubletas* then you should go and see the greatest expert on them – Luljeta Dano. And then you can see just what traditional Albanian silver was hung around.'

Like Linda, Luljeta had a studio in central Tirana, not far from Skanderbeg Square. I reckoned that if that woman on the mosaic took careful aim she could probably land a bullet on the doorstep. It was in the unappealing sounding 'Block' area of town which was once off-limits to all but the *nomenclatura*, and is an unlikely address to find a hoard of ethnographic and literal gold. I wondered how many other sidestreets in this city concealed secret entrances to the past. It was a thought that inspired me as I walked to meet Luljeta, reimagining the faceless concrete that dominated the cityscape as the solid walls of so many vaults, each hiding a treasure trove watched over by a tough enthusiastic woman of a certain age.

Luljeta wore her years lightly. She told me she was fifty, but she wore her black hair in a long girlish plait and she was vibrant in a paprika tunic. She offered me a hot drink and I asked for tea, which came fragrant with ayurvedic spices, and with it she brought a peach as bright as her dress. We sat down and she watched me eat.

Peaches are not an easy food to eat elegantly without cutlery, and I wondered whether it was a test as she surveyed me. 'You're not having anything?' I asked and she shook her head sadly,

'I need a coffee but I have an espresso machine for two, and since you wanted tea I'll go without.' A dribble of peach juice made its way sorrowfully down my chin.

I asked her about the *xhubletas* but she seemed to want to put off the moment. 'When you've finished your fruit,' she said, and I nibbled faster. Meanwhile we talked about literature – the room had a large bookcase and she was herself the writer of documentary film scripts and author of twelve books including poetry, a novel, a historical drama, ethnographic research and children's books with cultural heritage themes. She had previously been a journalist on the Albanian national broadcaster too. I told her about my books and what I was researching now.

'I want to have the freedom you have,' she sighed. 'I was born for books. These *xhubleta* have enslaved me. I've wasted so much time on them …'

'Not wasted, surely,' I said gently. 'You've *invested* all that time.' She shrugged.

'One day I won't be here –' it's interesting how my talk of ethnography led to talk of mortality '– and my daughter is 23 now and she's tired of my work with the *xhubletas*.'

It wasn't the introduction I'd expected but I told her how I saw these dresses fitting into my narrative – how my quest had started with the silverwork in the Prizren necklace, how it had taken me down mines and into dark workshops from Kosovo to Istanbul, 'and now I want to see how the craftsmanship connects with these traditions in Albania,' I ended triumphantly.

But I'd lost her at 'Istanbul'. There was an angry reaction that at first I couldn't understand.

'This,' – she gestured around her, at the studio and its treasures, but perhaps also at Tirana, at Albania… 'This is not Ottoman. For those of us who are Balkan Christians, Istanbul is Constantinople. The so-called Ottoman tradition of metalwork is in fact Byzantine and the metalwork you see around you is a continuation of ancient Illyrian and Celtic models.' She talked passionately about forced Ottoman conversions to Islam – 'shame on them.' She saw the Ottoman period as a blip – 'yes they were here for five hundred years, but what about before that? What about afterwards? Don't waste your time with Ottomanism,' she harangued.

I thought about her need for coffee; the Ottomans' was a blip that had left some deep cultural affiliations and addictions.

She went on to tell me the myth of Cadmus and Harmonia's three sons, the founders of the Illyrians, the Celts and the Gauls. 'Where are the Ottomans in that?' she asked in jubilation. I'd not heard this myth, and even when I went online later to that maker of modern myths, Wikipedia, I couldn't corroborate it, but her point was the connection of her culture with Western culture – deep down and way back.

'I believe in antique globalisation,' she said. 'People then had the same stories and the same symbols which linked them more than aeroplanes do today. That's what the *xhubleta* taught me.'

I'd finished my tea and my dripping peach. It seemed we could talk of *xhubletas* now. 'So tell me how you started collecting.'

She calmed with the memory of a story she was not telling for the first time, and the excitement of a rainy night. 'It was like a fairy tale,' she said. 'Oh, that rain – a complete storm. And someone gave me a sack with something inside it. They told me to take it and hurry home. With all that rain I didn't even have time to open the sack and see what it was, I just rushed home, worried that I might not make it, with the open drains and the problems in the streets.'

When she had got home she had found a *xhubleta* – she showed me a picture – embroidered with strange golden symbols in five thick bands around the skirt. It was an extraordinary image, and Linda's description of these garments as pages of a book came back to me. You couldn't look at this skirt and not feel you were in the presence of a code; a text. It could be Incan writing, or Egyptian hieroglyphics. It felt deeply pagan and significant, and yet utterly unknowable.

'It's from Kelmendi,' she said, naming one of the mountain regions that still felt remote even today. I wondered about this bride of Kelmendi stitching some kind of ancient knowledge into her skirts, transmitting information she couldn't herself understand; a mere channel for currents that run as deep as DNA.

'So that was the first; how many do you have now?' I asked, wondering whether she had the three that Linda had told me a poor bride would take with her to her husband's house, or the ten *xhubleta* of the rich.

From the xhubleta *collection of Luljeta Dano*

'I have seventy,' Luljeta said, sounding almost embarrassed by the excess. 'And around 800 pieces that form part of the costume. So let me give you a tour of a *xhubleta*,' she offered, taking me to meet the plastic mannequin who had been standing in an alcove behind us silently all this time, like an obedient Albanian daughter-in-law in her husband's family home. As if outlining the potential benefits of a match Luljeta pointed out all the woman's finest features to me. Our discussion focused on fortitude, strength, wealth, and good luck ….

The fortitude was shown in the intriguing pair of small tongs hanging on a long chain from the girl's waist. 'They were for lighting men's cigarettes,' Luljeta explained. 'The wife would use them to lift up a glowing coal from the brazier to put to the cigarette of her husband or of other men. Of course, for safety she would hold her other hand underneath in case the glowing coal fell. Then she'd be able to catch it. If that happened she wouldn't say a word; she was a mountain woman.' My eyes were watering. Luljeta said that Edith Durham had seen a link with the vestal virgins in this tradition of the woman of the house controlling the fire.

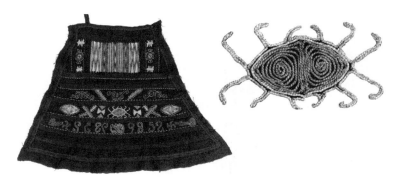

From the xhubleta *collection of Luljeta Dano*

Strength was shown in the very fact of the *xhubleta* and its sixteen kilograms of woolen weight. Luljeta repeated what Linda had told me about the dress needing to be sturdy enough to be able to stand up on its own and I thought about myself at eighteen, not a bride, but getting ready for my gap year travels, packing my first rucksack in Middle England's own rite of passage to adulthood. 'A good rucksack stands up by itself,' my worldly wise friends had told me, and I'd set the rucksack in my bedroom, daring it not to teeter over – with the same nervousness, the sense of being tested as to my readiness for the world, as perhaps that Kelmendi teenage girl had had.

But as well as the heft of the *xhubleta* there was an additional extraordinary weight, set round the mannequin's midriff like a shackle: a heavy leather belt, thick and glossy as a magazine and easily twenty centimetres high. The leather itself would make it as cumbersome as twisting *Vogue* round your waist, but what made this belt truly incapacitating was the mass of small studs, formed into a zigzag pattern reminiscent of the markings on an adder. 'This has ten thousand lead studs,' Luljeta said.

From the xhubleta *collection of Luljeta Dano*

In fact the word she used is the same as for 'nails' and I thought of each of these ten thousand hammered into the coffin of a woman's freedom. Luljeta continued with her tour, alternately doleful and excited by the craftsmanship. I remembered the word she had used for her relationship with these elaborate costumes – 'enslaved' and this did feel like a slave showing me round a museum of manacles. Looking at her bright summer dress I wondered whether her own choice of costume was significant too; her escape.

The costume she continued to talk me through was lavish. Even that stern belt was decorated with silver – surprisingly fine stylised eagles that had landed in the midst of the gothic lead-and-leather. Luljeta repeated what Linda had told me about silver's powers to defend against negative energy. She said that even if a woman had been rich enough to wear gold rings she would have made sure she had always had at least one of silver for its protective qualities.

Other silver was looped over and around the mannequin, in what Luljeta told me was traditional adornment as if these women had been very expensive Christmas trees. Silver would have weighed them down with amulets and brooches, long necklaces and triangular decoration on chains with further chains hanging off them. Luljeta pulled further items out of a bag (an IKEA bag, I noticed, with a wry meditation on competing forms of globalisation). The metalwork was fine though less lacy than I'd seen in Prizren. Here, it was not *filum* but *granum* which dominated the decoration. She showed me crucifixes which had at each tip a small paste jewel set in silver and surrounded by three twisted silver wires and then a double row of silver balls each in a starburst of fine wire. The paste jewels were all green and red and she said this is typical. They glowed like small traffic lights. A rich gold brooch studded with perhaps a hundred tiny gold balls as well as red and green jewels had a stylised silver bee set on it – a symbol of hard work and the sweetness that the bride would bring to the home, Luljeta explained.

The layers and encrustations of symbolism and of wealth were almost overwhelming. I returned to the quest that initially brought me here, thinking of that gun-toting woman on the National Museum frontage.

'Ah, the white *xhubleta* is for an unmarried woman,' explained Luljeta. She went to the sliding doors across the back wall of the room. Pushing them aside on smooth runners she revealed shelves stacked high with sleeping *xhubletas*. It reminded me of a morgue.

'The oldest one I have is 120 years old,' she said, 'but there's one in the Musée de l'Homme in Paris that's 300 years old. The most recent ones in existence were produced eighty years ago.'

Suddenly we were interrupted. Luljeta's attention had wandered, her eyes flickering manically around the room and her face hardening. I followed her gaze and saw what had so enraged her ... a small papery moth.

'My worst enemy,' she all but snarled. And of course if you were queen of the kingdom of wool then there was little that could do more damage. Feeling my place in that procession of history which I had seen on the mosaic in Skanderbeg Square I enlisted briefly in the army of the kingdom of wool, darting gamely around the room as the moth lifted and settled. Finally I got it where it hovered low in the shadows cast by a wooden wedding chest, and I stood up triumphant, rubbing my fingers. I had made a small contribution to Albania's cultural preservation, and finally Luljeta smiled at me.

From the xhubleta *collection of Luljeta Dano*

Chapter 12. Miss Mountain; Malësi e Madhe

'The best way to keep clothes free from moths is to wear them,' I was once told. I wondered whether Luljeta ever wore her *xhubletas*. I wondered whether anyone now wore a *xhubleta* … whether there was any surviving muscle memory of the experience of climbing into the dark depths of that heavy felt cone, like entering a diving bell, which had once been daily life for women across the Accursed Mountains. If not, what was done with the filigree creations that had been hung about them – the silver tracings which had outlined Albanian women for so many generations; where did those lines lead now?

'You can still see all that jewellery worn at the *Logu i Bjeshkave* – the "Mountain Meeting" – in Kelmendi,' I was told. This annual event apparently hosted a traditional beauty contest, choosing 'Miss Mountain' high up in the limestone peaks of northern Albania. I thought of bikini-clad lovelies in a landscape which clogs with snow for months each year. 'That sounds cold.'

'No,' my friend grinned, 'it's in summer. And anyway, the girls wear *xhubletas*. In fact the contest started as a competition between the girls of the village as to who had made the best *xhubleta*.'

So this would be my chance – to see a *xhubleta* not standing up on its own, and not just draped over the scuffed plastic of an old mannequin; to see how the tough wool carapaces moved with a woman within it; how the silver ornamentation I had been toured around in Luljeta's studio glistered in sunlight. I remembered Linda's analogy of the aquarium, and thought of the dead fish with dull eyes which you see laid in coastal markets along the Adriatic. Those had been the ornamented *xhubletas* I'd seen so far, but if I could get to Kelmendi I would get to see them swimming.

The journey would take me to a part of the mountain range where I'd not been before. I'd seen it only when I'd travelled to Montenegro and remembered it because of the enormous white cross picked out against the hillside. This was old Catholic territory, known for keeping to the old ways; of course this was where I could still see the *xhubleta* ensembles worn.

But first I needed to find out exactly where and when the Mountain Meeting would take place. Here again I discovered that the old ways – adapted to new technology – were still thriving. There was no information online apart from a home-knitted website which told me (as it turned out, erroneously), that the date of the festival was the second weekend in August. So I invoked the Albanian tradition of hospitality, the connections and intermarriage of clans, and its modern mapping through Facebook; I posted on social media a request for information. Within half an hour a friend from Tirana had suggested a restaurant in a village nearby the Meeting and where staff would be able to help, and I sent them a message.

They replied within five minutes with precise details of time and place. I was given more information about the origins of the Mountain Meeting, too – that it was a competition between all the women who had married in the last year. The restaurant's name was 'Bukë, Kripë e Zemër', translating as the 'bread, salt and our hearts' by-word for Albanian hospitality.

I was told that I could reach the Mountain Meeting by taxi or minivan from the northern town of Shkodra. 'Go to the 'Malësi e Madhe' café and there will be drivers who can take you,' I was assured. So now I was walking through the warm streets of Shkodra on an August Saturday afternoon. The pavements were thronged and many of the shoppers were in from the villages. I saw the characteristic neat white kerchiefs of the traditional Catholic dress, and old women with startling dyed black hair. I guessed that it was upcoming weddings which had multiplied the shoppers here – every purchase to be run past a trinity of decision-makers, with brides, mothers and sisters out together with their budgets. The fabric of every dress was to be rubbed between finger and thumb by three hands; the underside of every embroidered jacket to be picked at three times, every brooch tilted thrice to catch the light. I knew they would each return home rustling with cellophane. I nudged past shopping bags, forging my path to the roundabout where I was told that Malësi e Madhe should be, but it seemed to be taking a long time.

Ahead of me I saw a rucksack bumping along over tie-dye trousers and I wondered whether the fellow-traveller ahead might also be heading to the festival, or might at least have a map. I caught her up and asked in English whether she knew where she was going. It turned out that she hadn't heard of the festival, though she was interested in what I told her. Since she couldn't help me I was ready to move on, but it seemed that she wanted to talk.

'This is such an amazing place,' she said, wide-eyed. She was French and had been travelling around Albania for ten days. 'This morning I was thinking I might leave my job when I get back home,' she went on. 'I just want to come back here. I spent three hours early this morning waiting for a bus in Tirana and it was ... wonderful,' she murmured dreamily.

I smiled, marveling at the ways that the silver threads here entangle people, and I told her she should leave her job. She looked at me gratefully but quizzically, as if we were both mad. And since we probably were, and she also didn't have a map and she didn't know where Malësi e Madhe was, I lurched off again, wondering whether I'd missed the café. Eventually I stopped to ask an old man. 'Where's the Malësi e Madhe?'

His eyes were misty and he gestured with long waves of a trembling hand towards the mountains, 'Woah, it's a long way that way ...' he told me, so I kept going. After another ten minutes I stopped another man,

'You want the Malësi e Madhe? Are you in a car?'

No, no, I told him – on foot.

'Oooo, it will take you a long time. But keep going in this direction,' he pointed to the horizon, and I thanked him and continued on my way.

Five more minutes and I stopped a woman.

'For the Malësi e Madhe?' She seemed unsure. 'You mean the municipality or the café?' The confusion of my other informants started to make sense. The 'Malësi e Madhe' means the 'Great Highlands' and as well as being the name of a cafe it turned out it was an administrative area lying many kilometres to the north of Shkodra. No wonder the old guys had been dubious at the idea of me walking there.

Now we had established that it was the café I wanted the journey was not painted as such a tricky undertaking. It would be on my left at the next junction.

However, when I arrived there were no taxis or minivans waiting outside as I'd been promised. I walked up to the bar inside, explaining that I needed – with some urgency now – to get to some ornamented *xhubletas.*

'Sit down, si' down,' a guy offered me in Estuary English of glottal stops and flattened vowels. It was enough for me to guess at his history over the last eighteen years. I replied to him in English,

'Thanks a lot. Do you think I'll be able to get a taxi?'

'Yeah, yeah,' he assured me as he pulled out his mobile and summoned a number, starting speaking in Albanian.

When he was off the phone, I hazarded – feeling like Professor Higgins, 'Did you learn your English in London?' He nodded.

'I guess you went over in '98?'

He grinned in acknowledgement of what I knew. In 1998, at the height of the oppression that had cost Halil from Trepça his job, being a Kosovar Albanian was enough to ensure you asylum in the UK because it was so easy to prove the danger you would be in if you returned to Milošević's Yugoslavia. Many Kosovar Albanians had come to Britain then and their lives had been saved. At the same time Albania's economy had been in meltdown with the failure of pyramid schemes in which individuals and the government had invested heavily; what better way out for anyone able to convincingly claim that they were a Kosovar Albanian from just across the border. And so it is that many northern Albanians have Estuary English and many started learning it in 1998. This was the Balkans' other silver thread – the chink and glint of coins and notes earned on 'gurbet' which trails across a continent.

The phone rang and my fellow British citizen (he told me he was just back for the summer – 'seein' the faam'ly') sealed the deal for my two-hour journey to Lepushë with his mate Niku. I heard him at the end querying in Albanian, 'fifteen minutes? OK.'

He put the phone down and said to me in English, 'It will be ten to fifteen minutes.'

It was an inaccuracy, a misrepresentation of the facts I knew he'd been given. It was also a demonstration of his goodwill to me. He knew I wanted to see the festival and have the chance to see the silver jewellery on living display. I'd told him that I was worried about being late, so what he was saying in numbers was that he hoped I'd get there soon.

The taxi arrived in thirty minutes. I understood that with his estimate Niku the driver had simply been wanting to demonstrate to his friend, as his friend did to me, how keen he was to get the work. He had been explaining that he would really like to be at the café very soon. None of the statements had anything to do with estimates of time and motion.

Nevertheless, we were soon throwing down a challenge to time and motion and Niku was whisking me out of town and towards the silvered *xhubletas* of the Mountain Meeting. His car was comfortable and modern but he still opted for what he called 'God's air-conditioning' and the wind through the open windows whipped our hair into a frenzy to match the Albanian love-songs wailing on his stereo.

We exchanged pleasantries and I relaxed with him, grateful that we could communicate – Niku spoke the Gheg dialect of Albanian that I had first learned in Kosovo. The dialects are mutually understandable, but as an instinctive Gheg speaker I'm constantly wrong-footed when I speak to southern Tosks. In particular the past tense of my verbs has to be longer in

Tosk or standard Albanian, with an 'ar' added onto the end of each verb. It makes me feel like a pirate.

We were out through the suburbs of the city and then into the bounty of fields planted with olives and pomegranates, and chirring with cicadas and chicory, and then the homesteads became more scattered. Occasional signs for medicinal herb enterprises hinted at the forager economy here (this is a significant contributor to rural incomes: Albania is the world's largest exporter of sage, for example), and then fields became scrub and scrub became stone, and I thought that nothing could be foraged here; no-one could live here … Certainly no-one could dance in a *xhubleta* or jingle filigree jewellery here.

We were at the white cross now and I realised it wasn't, as I had assumed, created by cutting to reveal white chalk of the hillside, like prehistoric white horses in England. It was formed instead of hundreds of whitewashed stones gathered to form the cross laid out on the ground. It was the same technique that was used during the dictatorship to pick out slogans in vast letters across high ground. *Long live the party*, or *Long live the Proletariat*; *Together to victory with Comrade Enver*… I'd seen the film *Parullat* which tells the story of the slogans in one particular village and how the teacher who was threatening the status quo was given the longest slogan to form in these painted stones with his class of children, as a punishment for his insubordination. No-one would have dared paint stones in the form of a cross in those days when Albania was the world's first officially atheist state, but now people were putting their faith in something different from the Communist slogans when they lifted their eyes unto the hills.

Now we were off the main road and Niku ceremonially unclicked his seatbelt and simultaneously pressed his foot down on the accelerator. It was a contradictory set of behaviours, but I took it as a sign that we were now away from the city folk with their interfering ways, and we were into the wilderness where men could be men and cars could be fast and you trusted in God rather than the European Union's health and safety standards. I thought about testosterone and Albania's 'crisis of masculinity'; about the restriction of individuals' impulses, and I found I was still thinking about the *xhubletas*.

Despite the speed we were travelling at, I was still trying to take notes of the countryside we were passing through, and my hand leapt over the notebook like a polygraph. When he heard that I was writing a book, Niku was keen to share his knowledge of local history and the back-stories to the things we saw as we drove. He had lots of tourists he said – mainly Polish, Czech, British, Israeli, German and Italian – and he was clearly used to narrating the points of interest on the route: the cross ('done by someone back from America'), the large abandoned house ('belongs to the family of the head of the clan who converted to Islam in Ottoman times. He did it to save the rest of the clan from each having to convert, and the rest of them are all still Catholic'), the road ('asphalt just three years old'). But when I asked him about silver he was blank.

'Well, are there still silversmiths in Shkodra?' I asked.

'Yeah,' he said uncertainly, and I asked what they might make.

'Well, rings to order. And teeth.'

I started to have my doubts about this mountain ride. Was I to be jiggled for two hours up (and two hours back) to see a contest of parading girls showing off nothing more than rings and silver teeth?

'Er, have you actually been to the Mountain Meeting?' I asked Niku.

'I've been to Lepushë but not for the Miss Mountain competition,' he said. It reminded me that Miss Mountain was the name of my PE teacher at school. The incongruities of this enterprise multiplied.

And still we were making our way up the mountainside. I felt like a beetle in a quarry, inching up the vast stone walls. With bouncing and twisting the journey was not a comfortable one. I had hoped that it would at least get a little cooler with the increased elevation but the car thermometer was showing 32 degrees. I remembered the heft of Linda's *xhubleta* in my arms and marvelled that anyone would come up with the idea of wearing such a thing in this climate or on this terrain. We passed one of the infrequent signs with the name of a settlement. It said simply 'Hot.' I'd read the name of this clan before, but never had it seemed so appropriate. Later we passed the settlement of 'Stare' with an obliging arrow as if to show you where to look for the best view. At least, as the road became switchback, we never got to 'Pukë'.

And now we were at the top of a ridge and started to hurtle down the other side, all the way to the level of the river. Across the water the cliffs towered, as high as a citadel.

'That's Montenegro,' said Niku.

We were talking less now as it seemed there was less to talk about. The only things we passed of any note were an abandoned hut of barracks where I could still make out the words painted on the side – 'Enver' in confident capitals and 'Long Live Comrade Ramiz Alia', referring to Enver

Hoxha's successor. I pointed it out as a curiosity to Niku but he grunted. He said members of his family were imprisoned in that regime. He started on politics – the only time in the journey I saw him angry, thumping his fist on the dashboard with his passion about remembered wrongs.

The next thing we saw suggested we were getting closer. A man was making his way along the road towards us, his head shielded from the sun by some extraordinary homemade thatching. Small branches, complete with their leaves, were laid flat on the crown of his head in the same way I'd seen roadside stalls covered as makeshift shade. I knew from photographs that this improvised headwear was worn by the spectators at the Mountain Meeting; I guessed that he was coming from the festivities … perhaps just round that bend in the road …?

Soon the flow of traffic in which we had been a lone corpuscle was thickening and clotting, and as we rounded the mountain we could see the houses of Lepushë village studding the surrounding fields.

'I think we're here,' said Niku.

I got out of the taxi and looked around to try to orient myself. Where would I find silver *xhubleta* ornaments?

There were people everywhere. There was the smell of grilled meat from a field, and the sound of laughter from groups of men with beer around wooden tables some way off. But there was also the sound of music – the traditional songs of Niku's car speakers but amplified to fill a valley. I headed up the hillside and on a plateau found myself behind a stage where musicians were performing. Making my way round I saw who they were performing for – a crowd of perhaps five hundred sitting in relaxed groups on the hillside which formed a natural arena. They were people but if you squinted you could

believe that it was an animated hedge because almost all of them were covered with branches like the man we'd seen on the road. I never found out whether this was simple if twiggy practicality, or whether there was a Green Man heritage to the practice but the camouflage effect was unnerving. We could have been in a scene from Macbeth. Nevertheless, it gave an extreme rusticity to the scene; half animal half vegetable. I made for a free spot of ground, treading marjoram underfoot as I walked, so that the scene was infused with herbs.

The musicians were good but it was no beauty pageant; I wondered whether I'd missed the Misses. The next act came on stage and again there was no *xhubleta*. It was a young jazz singer dressed in a little black dress which I was betting she had not felted herself. She even apologised to the audience for her lack of traditional costume before starting the famous Highland aria *Baresha*, 'the shepherdess'. She was followed by a theatrical young man in traditional dress reciting verses from national poet Gjerg Fishta's 'Highland Lute'. It's a poem inlaid with silver, as it narrates not only the social but also the physical fabric of highland life and the heroes' and antiheroes' accoutrements – 'On one thigh a cartridge pouch all/ Styled in silver filigree with/ Trims and tassels dangling from it', the 'pipe of ornamented silver', 'a muzzle-loading flintlock/ Stock of which was silver-coated/ ... Even on a shelf 'twould scare you' (Robert Elsie translation). However, his costume didn't have the slightest gleam or glitter to it.

There was a sword dance which opened with a bit of theatre – a woman carrying one of the distaffs I'd seen on display at Linda's, and spinning the wool demurely was approached by an athletic young man. They simpered at each other and then a second athletic lad bounced on to the stage and drew his sword. The rest of the dance was the highly choreographed and impressive duel between the two men. The woman wound her wool determinedly throughout.

It was all charming stuff, but it wasn't what I'd come to see and I cursed Niku's timekeeping, realising that I must have come too late to see the women in their *xhubletas* after all.

But then, with the clashing conclusion of the sword dance the beauty contestants were announced and the stage was thronged with young women, each as carefully poised and adorned as Luljeta's mannequin. It was hard not to itemise them as they were presented for our assessment. They didn't wear sashes like the satiny slash of Miss World competitions – each instead had a yellow plastic disk pinned to her with a number on it. It's the same system used during the auctioning of livestock.

And so I officially disapproved, and yet I couldn't help myself ... that one had maybe slightly too fleshy a face; this one a nice smile; that one a neat sashay in her hips ... I tried to stop it. And I asked myself what I was doing anyway – I wasn't being asked to decide between these women. And what would I want with them? Men could be lured into this game with

a drool of sexual possibility, however hypothetical, but a 42 year-old woman like me …? I realised what it was – I was being invited to evaluate their value as daughters-in-law. I didn't even have a child of my own, and if I did of course I wouldn't select their partner, but I saw the anthropological role of madam I was filling here. I was doubly revolted at the process.

But it went on, even as I squirmed. Each girl stepped forward and presented herself with a short set piece. They gave their name and the valley they were representing and their age – between fifteen and 22. From these ages I presumed they couldn't be the brides married in the last year – it seemed more likely that this was a standard beauty contest with each valley having chosen a beauty to put forward. Then each said something sweet about what participation today meant to them. This is the iPhone generation: Snapchat, IM-ing, LOL-ing … and yet…

'My grandmother told me about this and through me the *xhubleta* will be bequeathed to future generations'.

'I'm here today because I want to experience wearing something that has resisted time,'

'For me the *xhubleta* represents other parts of our culture like the *cifteli* (lute) and our folktales'.

One of them recited a little poem, *Shqiptare me gjak, shqiptare me emër; Katolike me fe dhe malesore me zemër* – 'Albanian by blood, Albanian by name; Catholic in religion and highlander in my heart'.

I focused on what, after all, was the reason I had come – the silver. And there was plenty to see though I was interested that the designs on the *xhubletas* – that pagan silvering that had been narrated to me when the *xhubletas* were laid out in the studios of Linda and Luljeta – were obscured here, with the exception of those at the back of the skirts. The *xhubleta* was covered with a red cotton apron which was itself then covered with a black velvet apron, so the outfit echoed the colours of the Albanian flag. Were the pagan symbols only for private consumption then? Like lingerie.

Nevertheless, the velvet aprons were pinned with all the silver I'd seen before – a chain, reaching almost to the foot of the skirt, hung first with a crescent shape studded with stones, and from each point of which hung more chains each dangling a silver coin. The chain continued to a sunburst shape, from which swung more chains each ending in a coin. As the young women moved, the coins caught the light like the promise of plenty for the family lucky enough to net such a prize. Here the raw silver had a raw significance. On another girl's *xhubleta* the long chain ended in a filigree silver purse and off the purse jingled dangling ornaments. The repeated impression was that these girls were dripping with inherited wealth.

As well as these chains there was the decoration on the apron itself – here often much cruder than the old embroidery, in patterns made up of sequins rather than thread. In some cases this was also hung with coins – I counted forty on one girl. Gaiters were also festooned with chains and blotched with pinned or sewn metal ornament, or traced in metallic braid which made wandering patterns as if a snail had got lost here during the night.

But none of this was anything in comparison to the silverwork on the top half of the costumes. Each had the large heavy gold and jeweled cross which looked as much like a weapon as a religious symbol. It was slung from a chain under one arm, like a scabbard. On chains hung from the arms and the foot of the cross hung more coins; ready, presumably, to be rendered unto Caesar. On the belt were pinned one or more filigree brooches; round the neck was at least one, but sometimes three chains, a bracelet was at wrist, and rings around knuckles, and across the chest up to seven fierce brooches knobbled with metal and set with large stones. Some girls wore a metal breastplate set with stones and decorated with fine filigree spirals, flowers and zigzags. Heavy earrings swung from the earlobes and a silver comb was set in each girl's hair. Sometimes this, too, was hung with coins which jounced across the woman's brow as she moved. You would be forgiven for getting dollar signs in your eyes as you watched her. I thought of Gjergj Fishta again – 'Silver did her forehead shimmer/ Over eyebrows, as a mountain/ Over pathways shines in splendour'.

But what also came to my mind was Maisie in Henry James' novel, describing being embraced by her mother, pulled to her breast 'where, amid a wilderness of trinkets, she felt as if she had suddenly been thrust into a jeweller's shop-front.' It was a good reminder of the terms of this competition – even if the judges wanted to stare at the bodies of the women competing here, it was scarcely possible. Under the weight of *xhubleta*, the distractions of the gewgaws, and the multiple layers of aprons below and blouse and as many as four gauzy scarves above, only the basic body shape of endomorphs and ectomorphs was distinguishable. The heavy felt gave false hips to those who had none, and all the girls wore wigs with rows of tight pinned curls. With the make-up they wore, I wondered briefly in some cases where jaws were particularly heavy whether the contestants could even be men in drag. Like Maisie, you could hardly find a bosom under all that ornamentation, and thus it was made clear to the observer that we were not evaluating the flesh currently inhabiting the *xhubleta*; we were being invited to rate the encrustations which not only adorned but almost obscured her.

I wondered whether this was more or less weird than a beach babe bikini contest, and remembered that this started as a competition to judge the *xhubletas*, not the women who happened to be wearing them. They were as irrelevant to the traditional life of these highlands as the battered plastic of Luljeta's mannequin; it was the show of wealth they could make which mattered. The only qualities that soon become apparent in the women willing to carry all this silver about their person is their biddable nature and their stamina. For survival perhaps these were the traits which needed to be rated most highly for the Albanian woman.

Miss Mountain; Malësi e Madhe

Chapter 13. The worker bee future of filigree

A goddess, a worker, a businesswoman… Some rather more inspiring models of Albanian womanhood smiled down at me here.

I was in the shop and workshop of Krenare Rakovica in the centre of Kosovo's capital, Prishtina. I'd been told to visit her if I wanted to feel more positive about the future of filigree here – or about the future of Albanian women. Just a few doors along this street is the Pandora store selling status in the form of overpriced silver baubles in even more overpriced packaging. A little further on is the fool's gold of Swarovski. It seemed an unlikely culture and context in which the ancient art of filigree might flourish and yet Krenare's shop was busy. Not just with the multiple loops and chains and twists and finesses of the jewellery on display, but with customers. They were young women, sophisticated shoppers. A group who worked in the Central Bank had come in to look for a present for their colleague who'd just been promoted. 'It's beautiful jewellery, discreet and elegant,' explained one of them when I asked why they'd come here, adding the English word 'classy' to explain better what she meant. 'And you can wear the things Krenare makes even with your work outfit – it's not too fussy because she combines modern and traditional designs.'

Another girl was shopping for a gift for her cousin who'd just graduated. This was the tonic I needed after the images of womanhood available at the Logo i Bjeshkave festival.

Here were young women who worked in banks, who graduated, who 'leaned in' to celebrate others' successes … and who made filigree.

Krenare was the hard-working owner of this successful business and it seemed to me no coincidence that hanging from the walls of her shop was a picture showing a bee – that image of an industrious female that I'd seen also in Luljeta's collection of *xhubletas* and their ornaments. Alongside it was a plaque showing another strong female – the Neolithic goddess figure found in terracotta at sites around Kosovo and more widely in the region.

When I pointed these out to Krenare and asked her about her views on women in this craft she rejected any interpretation about modern girl-power. 'Women have always made filigree,' she said. 'I learned from my mother as well as my father, but my mother worked at it at home.' She reminded me about the women who work at the co-operative in Prizren too. 'The only difference is that as well as doing the filigree-making I also do the public-facing parts of the business.'

We broke off our conversation for another customer to make a purchase. She was young and smiling; another Kosovar woman looking comfortable and competent in a suit. I asked this woman too why she had chosen filigree.

'It's beautiful, and it's part of our traditions,' she said. She gestured around the shop, taking in not only the pieces of jewellery but also the Albanian flag and the striking photograph on the wall showing a bride from the Gorani region near Prizren. I'd seen the glitzy bridal costume from the region on display at the Ethnological Museum but I'd never been face-to-face with the extraordinary make-up which also adorned these brides. The base for the facepaint is white, on which sequins are stuck along with more silver

The worker bee future of filigree   151

threading in the form of metallic paint laid on in straight lines made using straws covered in pigment along their length and which covered the face – making repeated V shapes across the forehead and the bridge of the nose and to the point of the chin, as well as circles around the apples of the cheeks. The designs are said to keep away the evil eye. I remembered the spirals of my necklace which I'd learned at the museum were an Illyrian sacred symbol, and the triangular amulet – all echoed in shapes that Krenare had incorporated in her work. I realised that in fingering my necklace I wasn't just feeling a sentimental awareness of Rob's love and care – I was in a long line of women for whom the silver laid on us was a way of feeling safe.

Once the customer had selected her brooch and left, I was able to ask Krenare more about how she had reached the point of owning this business. Her name means 'proud' but in our conversation I found her strikingly humble – with no trace of the hustle that you'd imagine would be

needed to be a 'biznismene' (Albanian tellingly has no word for a businesswoman apart from a feminine ending on a transliteration of 'businessman'). But she was active – in between customers and while we were talking she sat at the workbench next to the sales counter and worked at some small pendants she was crafting which were also shaped like the Neolithic goddess. She showed me other pieces she'd designed too, where she had taken traditional forms and combined them in new ways – a brooch of layered paisley shapes infilled with distended spirals and set around a moonstone, a square pendant studded with sixteen punky 'granum' forms set amid coils and twists, and a leaf-shaped pin.

She had learned the traditions from her parents – a mother whose father is from Albania and a father who became a silversmith in the 'eighties. But when I asked her when she started learning she said she couldn't say because she had always played with the silver wire they'd had at home. There was a photograph framed on the wall which showed a young man in 1980s garb – a tank top and yellow trousers – sat cross-legged on a rug where he worked with tweezers and wire while a chubby baby looked on carefully. It was Krenare with her late father.

'Perhaps after my father died in 2004 it meant more to me,' she said. She had inherited his shop though it had been looted during the 1999 war and most of the tools had been taken. She picked up a pair of precision pliers and some wooden-handled tools – 'these were all that was left – basically just the *sican dish*.'

My ears pricked up. 'What did you call it?' I asked, looking at the tool she'd gestured to.

'This is a *sican dish* – it means 'mouse tooth', she went on. 'I guess it's called that because of the two nails that stick out.'

So one little linguistic conundrum I'd chased down from Prizren to Albania was resolved. I looked at the tool and its sharp protrusions which indeed could lead it to be named after little nibblers. So the *sican dish* didn't refer to the (tail) shape of the wire but the (tooth) shape of the tool that made it.

As I turned away from the workbench where her tools were laid out, my sleeve caught on the stand where she hung the pipe and nozzle for soldering the pieces. In Albanian tradition such a snagging means you have a debt to the person you're moving away from. As I disentangled my sleeve I mentioned the superstition to her and she smiled. But it was true – I was indebted for the new information but also for the freshness of Krenare's approach to her work.

She brought my attention back to the tools with wooden handles we'd been discussing, which were decorated with designs that reminded me of the motifs on the spindles that Linda had had on display in Tirana – the woodwork that she'd explained were given by lovers as a token. Krenare smiled, 'My father did that.'

Given her position in receiving these and so much more as a legacy from him and her mother, I asked what she saw as her own role in handing on the trade to others. Did she think there was a future for filigree, and for women in filigree?

'Women or men – it's all the same,' she said. 'It depends on there being help for people to learn.' It was the same thing I'd heard from Bashkim who was a generation older and on the other side of the country.

'You mean from the government?' I queried.

'No, not just the government,' she clarified. 'People like me can share how I make these things with anyone who's interested,' she said, and looking up at her wall again I reflected that she was talking now like a bee would. Perhaps rather than looking to institutions, this hive mentality is the hope for Filigree 2.0 in a time of crowdsourcing and outsourcing, of YouTube and blogging. Sitting in this shop was the first time I had begun to believe filigree might be able to survive here. As we talked I also noticed the significance of an Albanian verb we'd been using. 'Me bartë' is the verb for 'wearing' but also 'carrying' or 'transferring'; talking with Krenare had helped me see women's relationship with silver not just as *wearers* but also as *transmitters* of the power of this precious metal.

Chapter 14. Curation

My necklace had brought me further than I could ever have predicted. Following links in a shimmering chain I'd been led down the mines in Trepça and seen the rock where the shreds of silver glimmer. I'd learned the realities of life for the miners and how this search for silver had shaped Kosovo; its economy and society, and even its wars. On my desk sat the lump of sphalerite I'd been given at Trepça like the first clue in a true treasure hunt.

From there I'd seen how the landscape itself still bore the marks of silver even beyond the mines – tracing the humped dirt of charcoal burning that had enabled the ore to be smelted, and seeing the other shaping of the landscape that had come in the bunkers and fairways of Kosovo's abandoned golf course.

And just as the silver had wound itself through and around Kosovo, I saw how it was colonising me too. Now it was not just a light chain of spirals around my neck, but I had mouse teeth nibbling, and mouse tails swishing at my finger in that ring, an amulet to hang at my throat and silver glinting at my breast in the brooch from Mardin via Istanbul. My house now shimmered with Syzana's greetings cards and the intricacies of Pina's cigarette holder.

I wanted to write all this down and make connection with the place that this quest had begun.

So I went back to Prizren, birthplace of my necklace, and where I'd learned to parse the grammar of these threads. I thought of going to visit Mr Pasule, but when I asked about him Faik told me that he had died. And he shook his head when I asked whether there was a son or daughter taking over that business. There was now a hanging silver thread – the line which had connected seven generations over the blooming of fine metal flowers and which had now come to an end.

Thinking about indulging nostalgia I wondered about the original filigree factory. I heard from Faik that the site where I'd first rattled the butterfly gates in frustration when I'd lost my way was now a restaurant. It seemed like a good place to go and start writing down some of my adventures.

I enjoyed the confidence with which I approached the street this time, thinking back to my first halting visit years before. I looked out for the distinctive gates, wondering how the restaurant owners would have incorporated the filigree heritage into décor and menu. I had ideas for 'filigree carbonara' pasta, for bread rolls shaped into the rams-horn double scroll, for hot drinks served in glasses held in delicate silver lace.

The outside of the building did not immediately suggest that its new owners shared my enthusiasm for its heritage. The butterfly gates had gone, and as I walked through the yard I saw that the outside of the building was decorated with signs. Not exactly blue plaques – these were incongruous bon mots, as surprising for their pretended authors as for their location.

'If I had to live my life over I'd live over a saloon,' said William Shakespeare – apparently.

Inside there was evidence of the same eclectic approach. A vintage radio, a picture of Mother Teresa, whose family came from Prizren, together with images of national heroes Isa Boletini and Ismail Qemali. There was no filigree carbonara.

But it still felt like the right place to sit with my laptop and a cup of tea and to type up the story of my journey. I looked down the long room and imagined a younger Fatime, her hands tanned from her state-sponsored holiday, nimbly manipulating the threads of silver that had been spun from the bowels of the earth by the picks of Halil and his colleagues in Mitrovica. I thought of all the other women and men, from Mardin to Tirana and Prishtina, who'd bent in the same way to finesse such threads, and of all the men who'd bought their work and given it to the women they loved as Rob had done to me. I thought of the women who'd known the thrill I'd experienced as the fine craft slithered in a cool stream from the clasp. The journey was not just mine, but something shared by human beings through centuries.

It had taken me deeper in other ways – face to face with my fears, underground. And I'd got not only under the earth's crust but also under the skin of the countries which had produced the silver I'd tracked. I'd learned more about Kosovo's towns and cities; I'd travelled across borders to see how filigree was not only a phenomenon from within Kosovo but a part of a wider conversation with other countries of the former Ottoman Empire.

And in Albania, silver had given me a vocabulary for talking to people I would never have otherwise had the opportunity to learn from, including women long dead who had left behind their bright handcrafts, their ideas, their way of seeing and wearing the world. The journeys had given me a new understanding and a new lived experience of the fact that what we dress and adorn ourselves with shapes the world we inhabit. It offers us new ways to earn a living; new ways of being. It excavates our landscapes and helps to repel our enemies. It attracts our invaders, woos our lovers, and makes links with our friends. It explains us to our neighbours, to our descendants – and maybe even to ourselves.

A note on the pronunciation of Albanian

Albanian is an almost entirely phonetically regular language. This means that once you have learned the sounds made by each of the Albanian letters (very similar to English in most cases) you would be able to read a newspaper out loud – even if with very little clue of what it means.

For the Albanian words or names in the book, the following alphabet equivalences will be helpful:

A like *ar* in *card*

B like *b* in *bracelets*

C like *ts* in *bracelets*

Ç like *ch* in *church*

D like *d* in *delicate*

Dh like *th* in *with*

E like *e* in *ethnological*

Ë like *er* in *miner*

F like *f* in *filigree*

G like *g* in *gold*

Gj like *j* in *journey*

H like *h* in *history*

I like *ee* in *bee*

J like *Y* in *Yugoslavia*

K like *ck* in *rucksack*

L like *ll Y* in *all Yugoslavia*

Ll like *l* in *loop*

M like *m* in *miner*

N like *n* in *necklace*

O like *or* in *ore*

P like *p* in *paisley*

Q like *ch* in *church*

R like *r* in *rucksack*

Rr a rolled *r* that we don't have in English

S like *s* in *silver*

Sh like *sh* in *craftsmanship*

T like *t* in *twist*

Th like *th* in *thread*

U like *oo* in *loop*

V like *v* in *village*

X like *ds* in *cards*

Xh like *j* in *journey*

Y like the French *u* in 'tu'

Z like *z* in *zigzag*

Zh like *s* in *treasure*

If you enjoyed *The Silver Thread; A journey through Balkan craftmanship*, read Elizabeth Gowing's first book, *Travels in Blood and Honey; becoming a beekeeper in Kosovo* (Signal Books, 2011) available in Kindle and hard copy.

The book was described by *The Times* as

'A sheer delight; a beguiling, bittersweet story of a lively love affair with a traditional world, as ancient as apiculture, in transition to new nationhood'

TRAVELS IN
BLOOD AND
HONEY
becoming a
beekeeper in Kosovo

Elizabeth
Gowing

"enthralling... a wonderful evocation of a place that most of us know so little about. And I have every intention of trying some of the recipes." **Sophie Grigson**

Elizabeth Gowing's second book, *Edith and I; on the trail of an Edwardian traveller in Kosovo* (Elbow Publishing, 2013) is also available in Kindle and hard copy.

The book was described by *The Times* as

'The most delightful read of the summer'

Also by Elizabeth Gowing; *The Rubbish Picker's Wife; an unlikely friendship in Kosovo* (Elbow Publishing, 2015) is also available as a paperback, for Kindle and as audio.

The book was described by 'compelling and colourful' by Sophie Lam of *The Independent*.